SCHOOLCRAFT COLLEGE LIBRARY
W9-BXQ-110

Religions of the World

Buddhism

Christianity

Confucianism

Hinduism

Indigenous Religions

Islam

Judaism

New Religions

Shinto

Sikhism

Taoism

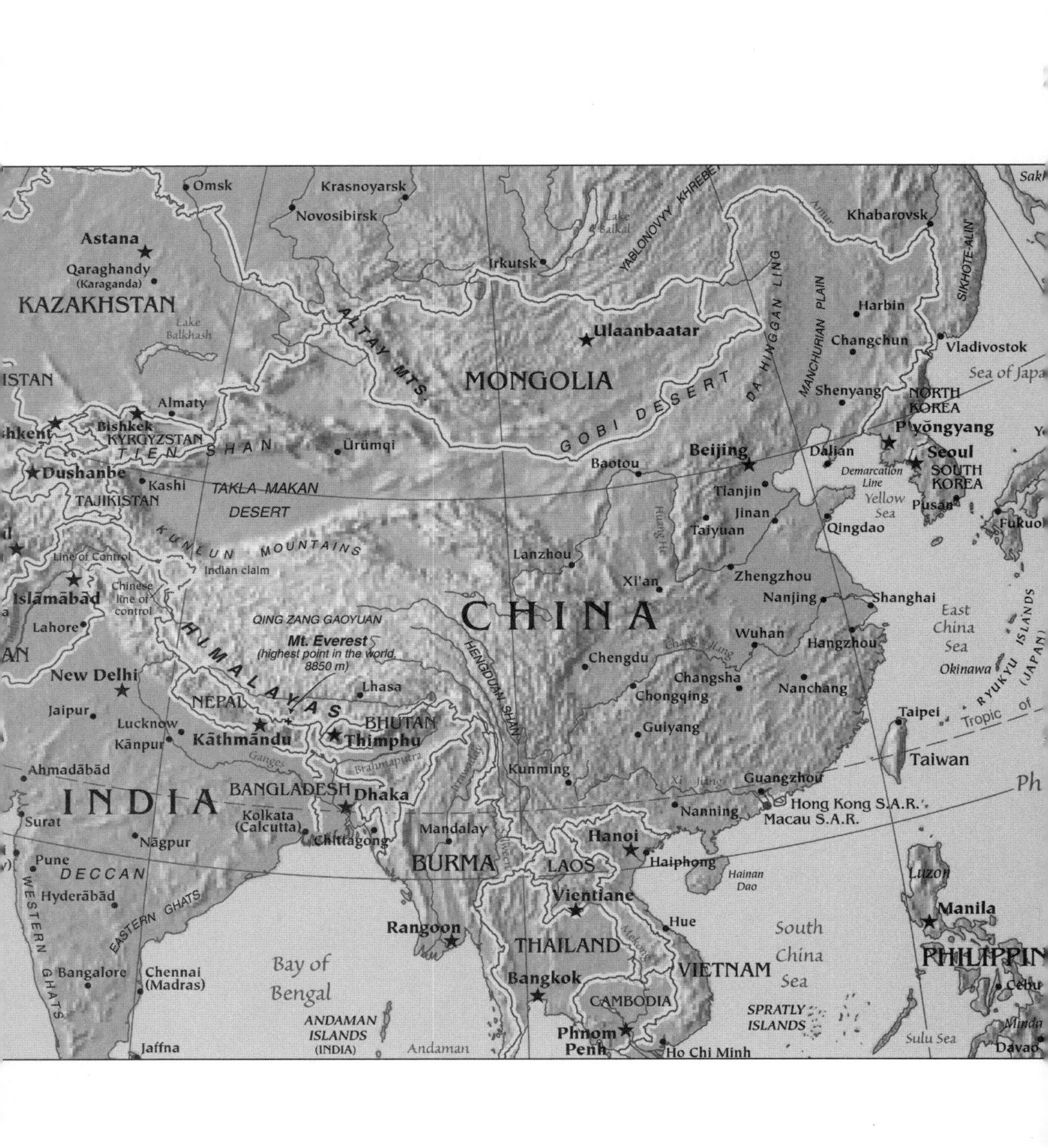

Omsk
Krasnoyarsk
Novosibirsk
Lake Baikal
YABLONOVYY KHREBET
Amur
Khabarovsk
Astana
Qaraghandy
(Karaganda)
Irkutsk
SIKHOTE-ALIN'
KAZAKHSTAN
DA HINGGAN LING
MANCHURIAN PLAIN
Harbin
Lake Balkhash
ALTAY MTS.
Ulaanbaatar
Changchun
Vladivostok
MONGOLIA
Sea of Japan
GOBI DESERT
Shenyang
NORTH KOREA
Almaty
Bishkek
KYRGYZSTAN
P'yŏngyang
TIEN SHAN
Ürümqi
Beijing
Dalian
Seoul
Dushanbe
Baotou
Demarcation Line
SOUTH KOREA
Kashi
TAKLA MAKAN DESERT
Tianjin
Yellow Sea
TAJIKISTAN
Jinan
Pusan
Taiyuan
Qingdao
Huang He
KUNLUN MOUNTAINS
Line of Control
Lanzhou
Indian claim
Zhengzhou
Islāmābād
Chinese line of control
Xi'an
Nanjing
Shanghai
CHINA
East China Sea
Lahore
QING ZANG GAOYUAN
HENGDUAN SHAN
Wuhan
Mt. Everest
(highest point in the world, 8850 m)
Chang Jiang
Hangzhou
HIMALAYAS
Chengdu
RYUKYU ISLANDS (JAPAN)
New Delhi
Lhasa
Changsha
Nanchang
Okinawa
Chongqing
NEPAL
Jaipur
BHUTAN
Taipei
Lucknow
Tropic of
Kānpur
Kāthmāndu
Thimphu
Guiyang
Taiwan
Ganges
Brahmaputra
Ahmadābād
Kunming
Xi Jiang
Guangzhou
INDIA
BANGLADESH
Dhaka
Hong Kong S.A.R.
Surat
Kolkata
(Calcutta)
Nanning
Macau S.A.R.
Mandalay
Nāgpur
Chittagong
Hanoi
Pune
BURMA
LAOS
Haiphong
DECCAN
Hainan Dao
Luzon
Hyderābād
Vientiane
Manila
WESTERN GHATS
EASTERN GHATS
Hue
Rangoon
South China Sea
THAILAND
Mekong
Bay of Bengal
Bangalore
Chennai
(Madras)
VIETNAM
Bangkok
CAMBODIA
ANDAMAN ISLANDS
(INDIA)
SPRATLY ISLANDS
Phnom Penh
Sulu Sea
Jaffna
Andaman
Ho Chi Minh
Davao

RELIGIONS OF THE WORLD

TAOISM

Hsiao-Lan Hu
and
William Cully Allen
Professor of Religion,
Temple University

Series Consulting Editor Ann Marie B. Bahr
Professor of Religious Studies,
South Dakota State University

Foreword by Martin E. Marty
Professor Emeritus,
University of Chicago Divinity School

Philadelphia

FRONTIS Prior to Mao Tse-tung and the Communist takeover in 1949, there were some five million practicing Taoists in China. However, over the subsequent three decades many Taoists were subjected to forced labor and torture, and were even murdered. By the 1980s, Taoism was thought to have been eradicated in China, but thanks to today's more liberal government, Taoism is again flourishing.

CHELSEA HOUSE PUBLISHERS

VP, NEW PRODUCT DEVELOPMENT Sally Cheney
DIRECTOR OF PRODUCTION Kim Shinners
CREATIVE MANAGER Takeshi Takahashi
MANUFACTURING MANAGER Diann Grasse

Staff for TAOISM

EXECUTIVE EDITOR Lee Marcott
EDITOR Christian Green
PRODUCTION EDITOR Noelle Nardone
PHOTO EDITOR Sarah Bloom
SERIES AND COVER DESIGNER Keith Trego
LAYOUT 21st Century Publishing and Communications, Inc.

A Haights Cross Communications Company

www.chelseahouse.com

First Printing

9 8 7 6 5 4 3 2 1

Library of Congress Cataloging-in-Publication Data

Allen, William, 1952–
Taoism / William Allen and Hsiao-Lan Hu.
p. cm.—(Religions of the world)
Includes bibliographical references and index.
ISBN 0-7910-8099-4 — ISBN 0-7910-8357-8 (pbk.)
1. Taoism. I. Hu, Hsiao-Lan. II. Title. III. Series.
BL1920.A55 2005
299.5'14—dc22

2004018405

CONTENTS

Foreword

Martin E. Marty

On this very day, like all other days, hundreds of millions of people around the world will turn to religion for various purposes.

On the one hand, there are purposes that believers in any or all faiths, as well as unbelievers, might regard as positive and benign. People turn to religion or, better, to their own particular faith, for the experience of healing and to inspire acts of peacemaking. They want to make sense of a world that can all too easily overwhelm them because it so often seems to be meaningless and even absurd. Religion then provides them with beauty, inspires their souls, and impels them to engage in acts of justice and mercy.

To be informed citizens of our world, readers have good reason to learn about these features of religions that mean so much to so many. Those who study the faiths do not have to agree with any of them and could not agree with all of them, different as they are. But they need basic knowledge of religions to understand other people and to work out strategies for living with them.

On the other hand—and religions always have an "other hand"—believers in any of the faiths, and even unbelievers who are against all of them, will find their fellow humans turning to their religions for purposes that seem to contradict all those positive features. Just as religious people can heal and be healed, they can also kill or be killed in the name of faith. So it has been through history.

This killing can be literal: Most armed conflicts and much terrorism today are inspired by the stories, commands, and promises that come along with various faiths. People can and do read and act upon scriptures that can breed prejudice and that lead them to reject other beliefs and believers. Or the killing can be figurative, which means that faiths can be deadening to the spirit. In the name of faith, many people are repressed, oppressed, sometimes victimized and abused.

If religion can be dangerous and if it may then come with "Handle with Care" labels, people who care for their own security, who want to lessen tensions and inspire concord, have to equip themselves by learning something about the scriptures and stories of their own and other faiths. And if they simply want to take delight in human varieties and imaginings, they will find plenty to please them in lively and reliable accounts of faiths.

A glance at television or at newspapers and magazines on almost any day will reveal stories that display one or both sides of religion. However, these stories usually have to share space with so many competing accounts, for example, of sports and entertainment or business and science, that writers and broadcasters can rarely provide background while writing headlines. Without such background, it is hard to make informed judgments.

The series RELIGIONS OF THE WORLD is designed to provide not only background but also rich illustrative material about the foreground, presenting the many features of faiths that are close at hand. Whoever reads all the volumes in the series will find that these religions have some elements in common. Overall, one can deduce that their followers take certain things with ultimate seriousness: human dignity, devotion to the sacred, the impulse to live a moral life. Yet few people are inspired by religions in general. They draw strength from what they hold particularly. These particulars of each faith are not always contradictory to those of others, but they are different in important ways. It is simply a fact that believers are informed and inspired by stories told in separate and special ways.

A picture might make all this vivid: Reading about a religion, visiting a place of worship, or coming into the company of those who believe in and belong to a particular faith, is like entering a room. Religions are, in a sense, spiritual "furnished apartments." Their adherents have placed certain pictures on the wall and moved in with their own kind of furnishings, having developed their special ways of receiving or blocking out light from such places. Some of their figurative apartments are airy, and some stress strength and security.

Philosopher George Santayana once wrote that, just as we do not speak language, we speak particular languages, so we have religion not as a whole but as religions "in particular." The power of each living and healthy religion, he added, consists in "its special and surprising message and in the bias which that revelation gives to life." Each creates "another world to live in."

The volumes in this series are introductions to several spiritual furnished apartments, guides to the special and surprising messages of these large and complex communities of faith, or religions. These are not presented as a set of items in a cafeteria line down which samplers walk, tasting this, rejecting that, and moving on. They are not bids for window-shoppers or shoppers of any sort, though it may be that a person without faith might be drawn to one or another expression of the religions here described. The real intention of the series is to educate.

Education could be dull and drab. Picture a boring professor standing in front of a class and droning on about distant realities. The authors in this series, however, were chosen because they can bring readers up close to faiths and, sometimes better, to people of faith; not to religion but to people who are religious in particular ways.

As one walks the streets of a great metropolis, it is not easy and may not even be possible to deduce the faith-commitments of those one passes unless they wear a particular costume—some garb or symbol prescribed by their faith. Therefore, while passing them by, it is not likely that one can learn much about the dreams and hopes, the fears and intentions, of those around them.

These books, in effect, stop the procession of passersby and bid visitors to enter those sanctuaries where communities worship. Each book could serve as a guide to worship. Several years ago, a book called *How to Be a Perfect Stranger* offered brief counsel on how to feel and to be at home among worshipers from other traditions. This series recognizes that we are not strangers to each other only in sanctuaries. We carry over our attachments to conflicting faiths where we go to work or vote or serve in the military or have fun. These "carryovers" tend to come from the basic stories and messages of the several faiths.

The publishers have taken great pains to assign their work to authors of a particular sort. Had these been anti-religious or anti–the religion about which they write, they would have done a disservice. They would, in effect, have been blocking the figurative doors to the faiths or smashing the furniture in the sanctuaries. On the other hand, it would be wearying and distorting had the assignment gone to public relations agents, advertisers who felt called to claim "We're Number One!" concerning the faith about which they write.

Fair-mindedness and accuracy are the two main marks of these authors. In rather short compass, they reach a wide range of subjects, focusing on everything one needs to advance basic understanding. Their books are like mini-encyclopedias, full of information. They introduce the holidays that draw some neighbors to be absent from work or school for a day or a season. They include galleries of notable figures in each faith-community.

Since most religions in the course of history develop different ways in the many diverse places where they thrive, or because they attract intelligent, strong-willed leaders and writers, they come up with different emphases. They divide and split off into numberless smaller groups: Protestant and Catholic and Orthodox Christians, Shiite and Sunni Muslims, Orthodox and Reform Jews, and many kinds of Buddhists and Hindus. The writers in this series do justice to these variations, providing a kind of map without which one will get lost in the effort to understand.

Some years ago, a rabbi friend, Samuel Sandmel, wrote a book about his faith called *The Enjoyment of Scripture.* What an astonishing concept, some might think: After all, religious scriptures deal with desperately urgent, life-and-death-and-eternity issues. They have to be grim and those who read them likewise. Not so. Sandmel knew what the authors of this series also know and impart: The journeys of faith and the encounter with the religions of others include pleasing and challenging surprises. I picture many a reader coming across something on these pages that at first looks obscure or forbidding, but then, after a slightly longer look, makes sense and inspires an "aha!" There are many occasions for "aha-ing!" in these books. One can also wager that many a reader will come away from the encounters thinking, "I never knew that!" or "I never thought of that before." And they will be more ready than they had been to meet strangers of other faiths in a world that so many faiths *have* to share, or that they *get* to share.

Martin E. Marty
The University of Chicago

Preface

Ann Marie B. Bahr

The majority of people, both in the United States and around the world, consider religion to be an important part of their lives. Beyond its significance in individual lives, religion also plays an important role in war and peace, politics, social policy, ethics, and cultural expression. Yet few people feel well-prepared to carry on a conversation about religion with friends, colleagues, or their congressional delegation. The amount of knowledge people have about their own faith varies, but very few can lay claim to a solid understanding of a religion other than their own. As the world is drawn closer together by modern communications, and the religions of the world jostle each other in religiously plural societies, the lack of our ability to dialogue about this aspect of our lives results in intercultural conflict rather than cooperation. It means that individuals of different religious persuasions will either fight about their faiths or avoid the topic of religion altogether. Neither of these responses aids in the building of healthy, religiously plural societies. This gap in our knowledge is therefore significant, and grows increasingly more significant as religion plays a larger role in national and international politics.

The authors and editors of this series are dedicated to the task of helping to prepare present and future decision-makers to deal with religious pluralism in a healthy way. The objective scholarship found in these volumes will blunt the persuasive power of popular misinformation. The time is short, however. Even now, nations are dividing along religious lines, and "neutral" states as well as partisan religious organizations are precariously, if not always intentionally, tipping delicate balances of power in favor of one religious group or another with doles of aid and support for certain policies or political leaders. Intervention in the affairs of other nations is always a risky business, but doing it without understanding of the religious sensitivities of the populace dramatically increases the chances that even well-intentioned intervention will be perceived as political coercion or cultural invasion. With such signs of ignorance already manifest, the day of reckoning for educational policies that ignore the study of the world's religions cannot be far off.

This series is designed to bring religious studies scholarship to the leaders of today and tomorrow. It aims to answer the questions that students, educators, policymakers, parents, and citizens might have about the new religious milieu in which we find ourselves. For example, a person hearing about a religion that is foreign to him or her might want answers to questions like these:

- How many people believe in this religion? What is its geographic distribution? When, where, and how did it originate?
- What are its beliefs and teachings? How do believers worship or otherwise practice their faith?
- What are the primary means of social reinforcement? How do believers educate their youth? What are their most important communal celebrations?
- What are the cultural expressions of this religion? Has it inspired certain styles of art, architecture, literature, or music? Conversely, does it avoid art, literature, or music for religious reasons? Is it associated with elements of popular culture?
- How do the people who belong to this religion remember the past? What have been the most significant moments in their history?
- What are the most salient features of this religion today? What is likely to be its future?

We have attempted to provide as broad coverage as possible of the various religious forces currently shaping the planet. Judaism, Christianity, Islam, Hinduism, Buddhism, Confucianism, Taoism, Sikhism, and Shinto have each been allocated an entire volume. In recognition of the fact that many smaller ancient and new traditions also exercise global influence, we present coverage of some of these in two additional volumes titled "Indigenous Religions" and "New Religions." Each volume in the series discusses demographics and geography, founder or foundational period, scriptures, worldview, worship or practice, growing up in the religion, cultural expressions, calendar and holidays, history, and the religion in the world today.

The books in this series are written by scholars. Their approach to their subject matter is neutral and objective. They are not trying to convert readers to the religion they are describing. Most scholars, however, value the religion they have chosen to study, so you can expect the general tone of these books to be appreciative rather than critical.

Religious studies scholars are experts in their field, but they are not critics in the same sense in which one might be an art, film, or literary critic. Religious studies scholars feel obligated to describe a tradition faithfully and accurately, and to interpret it in a way that will allow nonbelievers as well as believers to grasp its essential structure, but they do not feel compelled to pass judgment on it. Their goal is to increase knowledge and understanding.

Academic writing has a reputation for being dry and uninspiring. If so, religious studies scholarship is an exception. Scholars of religion have the happy task of describing the words and deeds of some of the world's most amazing people: founders, prophets, sages, saints, martyrs, and bodhisattvas.

The power of religion moves us. Today, as in centuries past, people thrill to the ethical vision of Confucianism, or the dancing beauty of Hinduism's images of the divine. They are challenged by the one, holy God of the Jews, and comforted by the saving promise of Christianity. They are inspired by the stark purity of

Islam, by the resilience of tribal religions, by the energy and innovation of the new religions. The religions have retained such a strong hold on so many people's lives over such a long period of time largely because they are unforgettable.

Religious ideas, institutions, and professions are among the oldest in humanity's history. They have outlasted the world's great empires. Their authority and influence have endured far beyond that of Earth's greatest philosophers, military leaders, social engineers, or politicians. It is this that makes them so attractive to those who seek power and influence, whether such people intend to use their power and influence for good or evil. Unfortunately, in the hands of the wrong person, religious ideas might as easily be responsible for the destruction of the world as for its salvation. All that stands between us and that outcome is the knowledge of the general populace. In this as in any other field, people must be able to critically assess what they are being told.

The authors and editors of this series hope that all who seek to wield the tremendous powers of religion will do so with unselfish and noble intent. Knowing how unlikely it is that that will always be the case, we seek to provide the basic knowledge necessary to critically assess the degree to which contemporary religious claims are congruent with the history, scriptures, and genius of the traditions they are supposed to represent.

Ann Marie B. Bahr
South Dakota State University

1

Introduction

The Tao (Way) that can be told of is not the eternal Tao;
The name that can be named is not the eternal name.
The Nameless is the origin of Heaven and Earth;
The Named is the mother of all things.

—Tao Te Ching, Chapter 1

Taoism is essential to Chinese culture. Taoist attitudes, ideas, and values have helped shape the minds and characters of millions of people in China, Mongolia, Hong Kong, Taiwan, East and Southeast Asia, Korea, and wherever Chinese communities have become established throughout the world. At least one fourth of the world's population is of Chinese descent, and the Taoist influence actually extends well beyond that. Not exclusive to Chinese cultures, Taoism has entered the mainstream of many Western societies, especially in the form of martial arts, *feng shui*, acupuncture, and *T'ai-chi*. A brief survey of book titles on Taoism for English readers demonstrates the popularity of Taoist ideas and practices throughout the United States. One on-line bookstore lists more than 4,500 English-language books on Taoism, indicating the extent that Taoism has entered American popular culture. Such books include:

Simple Taoism: A Guide to Living in the Balance
The Tao of Healthy Eating
The Tao of Healing: Meditation for the Body and Soul
The Tao of Daily Living
The Tao of Womanhood
The Tao of Music: Sound Psychology
The Tao of Bow Wow: Understanding and Training Your Dog the Taoist Way
The Tao of Leadership
The Tao of Pooh

A RIVER INTO WHICH MANY STREAMS HAVE FLOWED

"Tao" (or Dao) means the way, the road people walk on. More abstract meanings derived from this basic meaning include direction, rule, ideal, and the operating principle of the universe. The term Tao was widely used in various schools of philosophy in ancient China, and thus Taoism (often written "Daoism") is not the only philosophy to use this term. The "Tao" of the *Tao Te Ching* (Daodejing, Taoism's foremost sacred text) was actually only one of many understandings of the word in ancient China. However, just as the "Tao" of the Tao Te Ching is the original force that generates and encompasses all, the religious and philosophical system inspired by the Tao Te Ching has also demonstrated inclusiveness by incorporating many other ancient understandings of the word into Taoism itself. Taoism as we know it today has no specific founder and did not begin at any specific time. Rather, it has evolved with other elements in the Chinese culture that have helped to form and transform Taoism throughout time.

Due to its integral relationship with various aspects of Chinese culture, it is sometimes difficult to distinguish between being Taoist and being Chinese. Few Chinese-speaking people identify themselves exclusively as Taoists, yet much of their daily life involves Taoist beliefs and many of their customs are Taoist in origin. Many Chinese philosophies have their roots in Taoism, such as the movement systems of T'ai-chi (Taiji) and Ch'i-kung (Qigong), Chinese medicine and acupuncture, feng shui and the Chinese Zodiac, and ancestor worship. Taoism has been the source of inspiration for numerous Chinese poets and artists, including the "Immortal of Poetry" Li Po (Li Bo) and the "Saint of Calligraphy" Wang Hsi-chi (Wang Xizhi). Some imperial families publicly claimed to be the descendents of *Lao-tzu* (Laozi, who is presumed to be the author of the Tao Te Ching), while their court officials diligently pursued the Taoist ideal of immortality. Many of the revolutionary movements in Chinese history were set in motion by followers of various branches of Taoism. Taoism has interacted with and integrated many elements of what is now recognized as Chinese civilization, and, just as significantly, Taoism has brought these elements into the daily life of the people. Thus we can see that Taoism has grown and changed with Chinese culture and has become an integral part of Chinese culture.

Some scholars distinguish philosophical Taoism from religious Taoism. Their distinction is generally valid because Taoist philosophers do not necessarily worship like religious Taoists.

It is nearly impossible to find "pure" Taoism, philosophical or religious, because Taoism easily embraces and absorbs elements from other philosophical and religious traditions. For example, many Taoist ideas and practices are shared with other religious or philosophical systems, including the Ying-Yang school, Confucianism, folk religions entailing the worship of ancestors and immortals, and Buddhism. Professional Taoists (*Tao-shih*/ Daoshi), for instance, are often trained in Confucian ethics, and the most popular bodhisattva (a being who compassionately refrains from entering nirvana in order to save others) among the Chinese people, Avalokiteśvara, or *Kuan-yin* (Guanyin/ Japanese: Kannon), is recognized as one of the chief deities in the Taoist pantheon. Chinese folk religions have also blended

THE TRANSLITERATION OF CHINESE

The Chinese language is not spelled out using an "alphabet"; words are distinguished from each other mainly by their visual components rather than by their sounds. There are several ways to convert Chinese words into the letters of the Roman alphabet so that Chinese words can be spelled out and used in works written in Western languages. The converting process is called transliteration or Romanization. The Wade-Giles and the Pinyin are the most commonly used systems to transliterate Chinese into English. The former was developed by Sir Thomas Francis Wade and modified by Herbert Allen Giles in the late nineteenth and early twentieth centuries; the latter was developed by the Chinese government in the late 1950s and is gradually replacing all other transliteration systems. Both systems may cause confusion for speakers of American English. In some cases, the Pinyin transliteration may look more straightforward, such as the words "Dao" and "Taiji" (as opposed to "Tao" and "T'ai-chi" in the Wade-Giles system). At other times the Wade-Giles seems to make more sense, such as "Chang" ("Zhang" in Pinyin), "Ch'in" ("Qin" in Pinyin), and "ts'ao" ("cao" in Pinyin). In this book when a Chinese proper name is mentioned for the first time, both the Wade-Giles and the Pinyin transliterations are given so that it will be easier for readers to approximate the actual sounds of the Chinese words (the Wade-Giles is given first, and the Pinyin is written second or given in parentheses).

with Taoism. Therefore, the typical Chinese person is religiously eclectic and may embody the views and values of Taoism, Confucianism, and Buddhism in varying proportions.

A RELIGION THAT WAS NEVER FOUNDED BUT CONTINUOUSLY EVOLVES

As Taoism has evolved with Chinese culture, different elements have been incorporated into Taoism at various times. As a result, it is nearly impossible to single out one person as the one and only founder of the tradition or to identify one time period as the founding period. Chapter 2 introduces the life and times of four of the foundational figures of Taoism: *Huang-ti* (Huangdi), the legendary figure who is commonly recognized as the ancestor of all Chinese; Lao-tzu, the supposed author of the Tao Te Ching, the most widely read Taoist text; *Chuang-tzu* (Zhuangzi), to whom the work Chuang-tzu, the second most important text in Taoism, is attributed; and the "Heavenly Master" *Chang Tao-ling* (Zhang Daoling), the founder of the first religious Taoist organization.

Chapter 3 introduces the formation of the Taoist Canon (*Tao-tsang*/Daozang) and the most honored scriptures in Taoism, namely the Book of Change (*I-Ching*/Yijing), Tao Te Ching, Chuang-tzu, and the Scripture of the Ultimate Equilibrium (*T'ai-p'ing Ching*/Taipingjing).

Chapter 4 explains the concepts basic to a Taoist worldview, such as Tao, Yin-Yang, Five Elements, and the Taoist doctrine of nonaction and being one with Tao. Chapter 5 is a guided tour through the *Lung-Shan* (Longshan) *Temple* in Taipei, Taiwan. Taoist rituals practiced in the temple and at home are described. Chapter 6 describes Taoism in daily life, such as the Chinese Zodiac, feng shui, and the cultivation of vital energy (Ch'i/Qi) through Taoist breathing techniques and meditation. Chapter 7 discusses Taoist cultural arts, including calligraphy, painting, sculpture, music, architecture and literature, and the Chinese Zodiac. Chapter 8 describes Chinese holidays, especially the Chinese New Year, the Lantern Festival, and the Ghost Month.

Chapter 9 tells how Taoism evolved from one of the many philosophical schools to a religious movement among the commoners, then to a highly organized state religion that was used by the ruling people, and finally to an integral part of Chinese life. Chapter 10 discusses the Taoist ideals inherent in ecology, Chinese medicine, music theory, and religious inclusivism.

2

Foundations

To yield is to be preserved whole.
To be bent is to become straight.
To be empty is to be full.
To be worn out is to be renewed.
To have little is to possess.
Therefore the sage embraces the One
and becomes the model of the world.

—Tao Te Ching, Chapter 22

One of the early names for Taoism is "the method of Huang and Lao." The word "Huang" refers to Huang-ti (Huangdi; literally "the Yellow Emperor"), who is traditionally identified as one of the earliest rulers in Chinese history and the single most important foundational figure of Chinese civilization. There is no agreement as to the dates of the Yellow Emperor, but tradition says he lived about five thousand years ago. The word "Lao" refers to Lao-tzu (Laozi), who is generally recognized as the author of the Tao Te Ching (Daodejing), the most important work for both religious and philosophical Taoists. He lived in the Spring and Autumn period (770–476 B.C.E.) and was an older contemporary of Confucius, though the exact dates of his birth and death are unknown. The second most important work in Taoism is the Chuang-tzu (Zhuangzi), which is also called *Nan-hua Ching* (Nanhuajing) by religious Taoists. The author of the book Chuang-tzu is Chuang-tzu himself, who lived in the Warring States period (475–221 B.C.E.). Religious Taoism did not originate until more than three hundred years later. Chang Tao-ling (Zhang Daoling) established the first religious organization of Taoism called the "Five Pecks of Rice Tao" during the Eastern Han dynasty (25–220 C.E.). Today all Taoists, whether professional or lay, still revere Chang Tao-ling (Zhang Daoling) as Chang T'ien-shi (Zhangtianshi)—meaning the "Heavenly Master Chang."

HUANG-TI: THE COMMON ANCESTOR OF THE CHINESE PEOPLE

Huang-ti and another legendary ancient ruler, Yen-ti (Yandi), are publicly recognized as the most important foundational figures of Chinese civilization. They are deemed the ancestors of the Chinese people; this is why Chinese people frequently refer to themselves as "the descendants of Yen and Huang." From as early as the Han dynasty (206 B.C.E.–220 C.E.), legends about Huang-ti abound. In one of those legends, Huang-ti's mother went to a field, where she witnessed a huge flash of lightning encircling the first star of the Great Dipper; immediately she became pregnant with Huang-ti. In a Taoist hagiographical book (a biography of venerated people) called *The Record of Immortals* (*Lieh-hsien chuan*; *Liexianzhuan*), Huang-ti is presented as the leader of hundreds of deities. He is revered as a deity, and many Taoist scriptures were attributed to him, such as the Talisman Scripture of Huang-ti (Huang-ti yin-fu ching/Huangdi yinfujing) and the Dragon-Head Scripture of Huang-ti (Huang-ti lung-shou ching/Huangdi longshoujing); although in fact these scriptures were written much later, sometime after the beginning of the Common Era.

Huang-ti is highly honored because many cornerstones of Chinese civilization were established during his lifetime. According to tradition, he united all the tribes of ancient China under his rule. The method of dividing time into cycles of sixty years, which is still in use today, was established during his day (see the sidebar in chapter 6 for more details about the sixty-year cycle). Huang-ti is recognized for the invention of bows, arrows, boats, and carts. He was also the first to build houses for people to live in (so that they no longer lived in caves or trees). His wife, Lei-tsu (Leizu), was the first to breed silkworms so that people

THE SIGNIFICANCE OF THE PRE-CH'IN (PRE-QIN) ERA IN CHINESE PHILOSOPHY

In addition to philosophical Taoism, there were many other schools that either took shape during the Eastern Chou dynasty (the Spring and Autumn period and the Warring States period) or had their roots in earlier times but were more systematically developed at this time. Among those schools are Confucianism, Legalism, Agriculturalism, Logicians' Thoughts, Yin-Yang, and the Five-Element Theories, all of which continue to influence Chinese culture to some degree or another. That is to say, whichever period of Chinese history a researcher intends to focus on, one must study these schools as background knowledge. Since all of these schools were formed prior to the establishment of the Ch'in dynasty (221–206 B.C.E.), they are usually collectively called the Pre-Ch'in schools, and the Pre-Ch'in era has been considered one of the golden eras in the history of Chinese philosophy.

could make clothes out of silk, and one of his high officials, Ts'ang-chieh (Cangjie), established the Chinese writing system. Another of his officials established the five basic keys and twelve pitches of Chinese music, and invented the first Chinese bamboo flutes. Huang-ti also discussed pathology with the court doctor and laid the foundations for Chinese medical theory by writing the Inner Scripture of Huang-ti (although archaeological evidence suggests that the book was actually written much later, during the Han dynasty). Huang-ti also invented the compass and, according to legend, used it to direct his army through a dense fog produced by a witchdoctor loyal to Ch'ih-yu (Chiyou), chief of a warring tribe, and defeat him.

LAO-TZU: THE WISE ELDER IN A GAIN-CRAZED SOCIETY

Another figure revered as a deity by Taoists is Lao-tzu. His surname is Li, and he had two given names, one of which is Er, meaning "ear," in Chinese, and the other is Tan (Dan), which indicates the rims of his ears were flat rather than curly. One story says Lao-tzu had an exceedingly long life as a result of his self-cultivation, and that is why he was called Lao-tzu, "the honorable elder," with "lao" meaning "elder," and "tzu" being an honorific suffix in Chinese that was used to show respect. (The words "Confucius" and "Mencius" are the Romanized rendering of K'ung-tzu/Kongzi and Meng-tzu/Mengzi, with "tzu" as the honorific suffix.) According to another legend, Lao-tzu was conceived in his mother's womb by a shooting star. After becoming pregnant with Lao-tzu, his mother carried him in her womb for eighty years. According to this fanciful account, Lao-tzu was born already old, wrinkled, and with long white hair and a beard.

The era during which Lao-tzu lived is called the Spring and Autumn period, which was during the first half of the Eastern Chou dynasty (770–221 B.C.E). It was during this time that the centralized feudal system of the Chou (Zhou) dynasty started to fall apart. At the beginning of the Chou dynasty, the whole territory was divided into many small fiefs or states and assigned to dukes, marquises, earls, viscounts, and barons as their domains. Those patricians were the lords within the range of their own fiefs, but officially they were still ruled by the king of the Chou and were still expected to recognize him as the central political authority. When the king of the Chou dynasty moved the capital eastward in 770 B.C.E. (hence the term "Eastern Chou"), due to the significant threat presented by an ethnic group living around the western border of Chou, things started to change. Apparently the king was too weak to defend the dynasty against raids by that group, which also meant he was not a formidable central leader anymore. Consequently, feudal lords became less subordinate and more assertive. A few of the dukes even battled with the Chou army or forced the king of the Chou to publicly acknowledge their dominant role among the feudal lords, though they still officially recognized him as the king. On the other hand, the dukes bullied one another and demanded tribute from their fellow feudal lords who did not possess as much military power. Quite simply, this was an era of much distress and disorder.

Lao-tzu was sick and tired of a society where people were obsessed with power and gain, where people resorted to force in order to establish themselves, and where people felt good only when they subordinated others. Fed up with society, Lao-tzu decided to leave the territory of the Chou. According to legend, Lao-tzu mounted a water buffalo and rode off westward into the sunset. As he reached the border of Chinese civilization, he was stopped by a guard at Han-ku (Hangu), one of the passes along the western border of the Chou dynasty. This border guard somehow knew that Lao-tzu was profoundly wise and that it would be the general public's loss if Lao-tzu simply left without first imparting his wisdom; therefore the guard pleaded with Lao-tzu to write something down. Lao-tzu was reluctant to do so and only consented under duress; the border guard simply would not let Lao-tzu cross unless he wrote down his wisdom. Within hours Lao-tzu composed a highly condensed text of about five thousand Chinese characters. This text is the Tao Te

Ching, and most Chinese people consider it a work of political philosophy rather than a religious work (see chapter 3 for a discussion of the Tao Te Ching).

CHUANG-TZU: AN ALTERNATIVE WAY OF FACING DEATH

If the Spring and Autumn period was disorderly, the Warring States period was total chaos. As the name suggests, this was a time of wars. From 475 to 221 B.C.E., there were a total of 230 wars, involving hundreds of thousands of soldiers. The king of Chou was entirely powerless because his domain was smaller than most of the feudal lords' domains. Some feudal lords blatantly exceeded the former hierarchical boundaries and started to call themselves kings. Invading one another's domain had become a common practice among the feudal lords, and, as a result, many of the previous states were demolished. Moreover, some of the patricians of lower status who formerly served as the court officials in those feudal states deployed every means to rise in power, even developing their own armies. They fought with each other fiercely, continued to invade and claim other areas, and either imprisoned their own lords or executed them. When the Eastern Chou dynasty began in the Eighth Century B.C.E., there were 128 states, and by the middle of the Fourth Century B.C.E., only seven remained. Needless to say, countless people died in the wars of this turbulent time.

Chuang-tzu lived during the Warring States period. He saw people literally die at any moment because of constant wars. In response, he emphasized the importance of life and taught techniques for protecting one's own life. An anecdote in the book Chuang-tzu describes how some trees grow extraordinarily tall and strong and beautiful, while others are ugly and gnarled. Public opinion would likely praise the beauty and usefulness of the former, and pity the latter and consider them pathetic. However, as soon as those "useful" trees reached a certain size, they were chopped down; in contrast, the seemingly pathetic, gnarled trees would never be chopped down and could live forever, precisely because they were totally "useless." Over-achievers are in fact harming themselves; in contrast, those who do not desire praise and do not show off their abilities can live happily forever. With no end of war in sight, Chuang-tzu developed a "let it go" attitude and a "being one with nature" philosophy that is reflected in the stories about his life. In one of the stories, Chuang-tzu's wife died, and his friend found him squatting on the ground, beating a basin as a drum and singing. His friend questioned him: "When someone who has lived with you and raised children for you grows old and dies, isn't it insensitive enough that you do not shed any tears? How can you possibly be beating the basin and singing?"[1] Chuang-tzu replied that he was happy about the fact that his wife had returned to nature; her death was a loss only from the perspective of a human, and human perspective is petty and cannot take into consideration the necessary and beneficial circularity of nature.

CHANG TAO-LING: THE FIRST RELIGIOUS TAOIST

Huang-ti was supposedly the first religious Taoist, but he is a legendary figure, and none of the stories about his life and achievements can be corroborated. The historical Lao-tzu and Chuang-tzu were philosophers with very unusual ideas. Neither of them presented themselves as religious leaders, and there was no evidence of them being religious even though in later times Lao-tzu was revered as a deity and Chuang-tzu was considered an immortal. In the second century B.C.E., the ruling class claimed to be practicing "the method of Huang and Lao"; this meant that they would dedicate themselves to the public welfare following Huang-ti's example, and they would carry out Lao-tzu's instructions of not meddling with the commoners' lives by imposing unnecessary policies. Around the same time, there also emerged a cult called "Huang-Lao Tao," but it had nothing to do with ruling or politics. Rather, it incorporated popular beliefs, and its specialists were mediums, sorcerers, and magicians. The primary concern of this cult was the pursuit of long life. The political philosophy of Lao-tzu and the popular religious beliefs and practices were still readily distinguishable. Taoism as an organized religion that incorporates the philosophies of Lao-tzu and Chuang-tzu was not founded until the second century C.E. Oddly enough, the founder for this organized religion was neither Lao-tzu nor Chuang-tzu, but Chang Tao-ling.

According to tradition, Chang Tao-ling grasped all the subtleties of the Tao Te Ching at the age of seven and was also well educated in the Five Classics of Confucianism. Since he was eager and determined to learn more about Tao, he gave up the path of serving as a Confucian scholar-official and went into the southwest mountains of the Eastern Han dynasty to seek the Tao. Tradition claims he was quite a magician; he could suddenly disappear while sitting in front of others and then emerge from the middle of a pond. He could also show up in different places simultaneously; for example, at the same time, people saw him reciting scriptures in the hall, entertaining guests by the table, and walking alone with a walking stick in hand composing poetry. In addition, he could command the mountain deities. Tradition records that he met Lao-tzu (already deified by this time) on a mountain, and Lao-tzu taught him how to prepare a medicine that could render him immortal. Holding the secret to immortality, Chang Tao-ling was nevertheless concerned about the life of the common people; therefore he founded a religious organization, created various talismans, and subdued or dispelled malicious spirits for the followers. He also taught the followers to repent for their misbehavior, to practice self-moderation, and to contribute to the public welfare by paving roads, building public shelters, feeding travelers, and so on. Since members were required to hand in five pecks of rice as the membership fee, the organization was commonly called the "Five Pecks of Rice Tao." The founding figures' thoughts are described further in chapters 3 and 4, and more on the history of Taoism is found in chapter 9.

3

Scriptures

Being and non-being produce each other;
Difficult and easy complete each other;
Long and short contrast each other;
High and low distinguish each other;
Therefore the sage manages affairs without action
And spreads doctrines without words.

—Tao Te Ching, Chapter 2

Contrary to popular opinion, the earliest Taoist scripture is not Lao-tzu's text the Tao Te Ching (Classic of the Way and Its Power). To be sure, the Tao Te Ching is the foundation of philosophical Taoism and has deeply affected religious Taoist thought as well, but it is not the first book of importance to Taoism. Widespread Taoist beliefs and practices, such as feng shui (including the practice itself and the theory behind that practice), have their roots in the I-Ching (Yijing; the Book of Change), a scripture written sometime around the beginning of the Western Chou dynasty (1050–771 B.C.E.). Another foundational work of philosophical Taoism is the Chuang-tzu. The earliest religious Taoist scripture available is T'ai-p'ing Ching (Taipingjing), the Scripture of the Ultimate Equilibrium. This scripture appeared around the turn of the second century C.E., and the rapidly spreading religious Taoist organization was named after it and called T'ai-p'ing Tao (see chapter 9). By the time of the T'ang (Tang) dynasty (618–907 C.E.), there were so many scriptures of religious Taoism that one of the T'ang emperors ordered them all sequenced and compiled into what is called the Taoist Canon (Tao-tsang/Daozang).

I-CHING (BOOK OF CHANGE)

The Chinese character for the "I" in I-Ching has many meanings; it can mean easy, simple, change, or exchange. In fact, those meanings are the focus of this scripture. The I-Ching uses some very simple and easy-to-remember symbols to reveal the ever-changing nature of the world, how things will change, and what it takes to make things move toward a desired end. The original hieroglyph of the character depicted a lizard, which could change its color and adapt to the environment in order to protect itself. The I-Ching is also a book that teaches how to recognize opportune moments in life to make adaptations and changes. The I-Ching is also a Confucian scripture—it is one of the Five Classics of Confucianism, and almost all of the versions available today include the interpretations of Confucius. This book was very much revered by Confucius, who once said, "Give me a few more years so that I can devote fifty years to study Change (I-Ching), then I may be free from great mistakes."[2] The fact that Taoism and Confucianism share a scripture partially explains why Taoism and Confucianism easily converged later in Chinese history (see chapter 9).

The basic components of the I-Ching are Yin and Yang. Yin is represented by a horizontal line divided in the middle, while Yang is represented by an undivided horizontal line. The Eight Trigrams (*pa-kua*/bagua) are composed when any three lines, either the Yin symbol or the Yang symbol, are put on top of one another. The Eight Trigrams stand for sky, earth, mountain, lake, thunder, wind, fire, and water (see "The Eight Trigrams" sidebar on page 19 and Web site on page 98). The sixty-four hexagrams are made when any two of the Eight Trigrams are put on top of one another. The I-Ching provides a general explanation for each hexagram and a separate explanation for each Yin or Yang symbol, analyzing that symbol's significance in relation to the whole hexagram. In each set of hexagram explanations, the first symbol explained is always the bottom one, and an expert I-Ching scholar, when drawing any hexagram, always starts with the bottom line and then moves up line by line. The philosophy behind the I-Ching is that every situation has its root and that to understand any situation one has to examine how and under what condition it started.

It is possible that the sixty-four hexagrams originally carried meanings in reference to practical matters. Consider the possibility that two groups of people were traveling on the same route, and the first group encountered mountain torrents. It was impossible to pass through that area, so the group went back to a certain point and drew on the road the hexagram *Difficulty* (Chien/Jian; the hexagram's name), with the trigram *Mountain* at the bottom and the trigram *Water* on top. Consequently, a second group also wishing to proceed along the road would know there was water flowing down the mountain and change their route for their own safety. Of course, a concrete meaning like this would make sense only in a society where life centered on people's interactions with nature. Each hexagram also has many layers of derived abstract meanings, which have been applied in politics, logistics, education, Chinese medicine, and mystical quests. The I-Ching is one of the most influential and most frequently consulted works in Chinese history.

TAO TE CHING (CLASSIC OF THE WAY AND ITS POWER)

As stated in chapter 1, the word "Tao" simply means the way and is extended to mean direction, rule, ideal, or the operating principle of the cosmos. The word "Te/De" can mean power, application, or virtue. As the different meanings of the word "I" are suggestive of what the I-Ching encompasses, the multiple meanings of both "Tao" and "Te" are very suggestive, too: They imply that one who applies the power of the operating principle of the cosmos to life will have a sense of direction and obtain virtue. The Tao Te Ching is therefore a book about the truth of the universe and how its power can be applied to life. This book contains eighty-one very short chapters, with the first thirty-seven grouped under the word Tao and the remaining forty-four grouped under the word Te. Due to its brevity, the language

THE EIGHT TRIGRAMS

The trigram with three undivided lines stands for the sky or heaven, and the trigram with three divided lines indicates the earth or ground. The trigram with one undivided line at the bottom and two divided lines on top is the symbol for thunder, and the trigram with two divided lines at the bottom and one undivided line on top stands for a mountain. The trigram with two undivided lines between one divided line stands for fire, and the trigram with two divided lines between one undivided line stands for water. The trigram with two undivided lines at the bottom and one divided line on top stands for a lake, and the trigram with one divided line at the bottom and two undivided lines on top stands for the wind. Heaven, earth, thunder, mountain, fire, water, lake, and wind were apparently what the ancient Chinese people considered to be the most important elements in their life.

appears to be quite cryptic. This cryptic quality makes the text read like a mystical book; however, most Chinese people regard the Tao Te Ching as a political philosophy text, because the word "Sage" (*Sheng-jen*/Shengren) appears in the text frequently and almost always refers to "the ideal ruler."

As stated in chapter 2, Lao-tzu lived in an era that was very turbulent, and he thought the main problem was that most people, particularly the rulers, were obsessed with establishing something magnificent in the hope of acquiring fame. According to Lao-tzu's assessment, rulers were obsessed with setting up norms and then using force to impose those norms on others with the hope that the world would operate according to the ruler's wishes. A typical ruler was concerned only with elevating his own status by subjecting others to his authority. The "Sage," on the contrary, would model himself after the Tao that has been the mother and the nurturer of the myriad of things in the universe without ever claiming her authority or possession. Just as the Tao has treated the myriad of things equally without favoring one over the others, the "Sage" does not honor only one specific set of personality traits, uphold only one set of norms, or value only certain goods while denouncing all others. As Tao has let the myriad of things be themselves, the "Sage" does not elevate his own ideology to the absolute or impose it on the people, nor does he try to enforce his own ideology with military power. In sum, the best way to rule is to do what Tao has always been doing.

In addition to its contribution to political thought, the Tao Te Ching is also known for its delineation of the circular movement of a mystical, infinite, and profound origin from which all things sprang. The Tao Te Ching likens the operating principle of the universe to a mother. It claims that systematic knowledge falls short of grasping the whole complexity of reality. It teaches the benefit of being humble and thinking humbly, and it councils self-preservation by avoiding risks and adapting to circumstances. Chapter 4 will address the Tao Te Ching's worldview in more detail.

CHUANG-TZU/NAN-HUA CHING

Although named after the philosopher Chuang-tzu, scholars suspect that Chuang-tzu (also called Nan-hua Ching) may actually be a collection of the writings of a group of thinkers rather than representing one person's voice. Many scholars believe that only the seven Inner Chapters were written by Chuang-tzu himself, and that the fifteen Outer Chapters and eleven Mixed Chapters were written by his disciples and followers. Some speculate that the distinction between the Inner, the Outer, and the Mixed Chapters was merely imposed by an anonymous editor. Whatever the case may be, the content of Chuang-tzu is mostly treated as an integral whole, and when citing from the book, people still use "Chuang-tzu said . . . ," rather than "Chuang-tzu the book said . . ."

Chuang-tzu shared most of Lao-tzu's concerns and often exceeded them. Like Lao-tzu, Chuang-tzu emphasized self-preservation; however, Chuang-tzu was much more emphatic in stressing the importance of self-preservation. This is understandable because in Chuang-tzu's time, society had degenerated from disorder to the total chaos of the Warring States period. According to Lao-tzu, the root of disorder in the Spring and Autumn period was that people too frequently established norms according to their own understanding and then wanted to impose them on others by force. Chuang-tzu agreed with this viewpoint and said that people did so because they were trapped in a conventional way of thinking. People often note differences between things, and part of the socialization process teaches them to classify those differences using categories predetermined by others. This reinforces the apparent reality of the differences, and the unity behind the multiplicity is ignored. The wind can hoot, hiss, sniff, suck, mumble, moan, whistle, and wail, and it can go through pipes and tubes and produce a chorus. People hear various sounds and identify those sounds as distinct without understanding that they are all the results of the flow of air.[3] Tao is spontaneous and incessantly transforms itself, and it may produce and nurture millions and millions of differences in its constant flux, but ultimately there is just one Tao.

Rather than developing a political philosophy, as Lao-tzu had done, Chuang-tzu turned inward and depicted a limitless world of imagination and liberation that would be brought about by shaking off the limits of conventional categorization and by realizing the unity of all things. From Chuang-tzu's point of view, the various schools at his time were all myopic in that they saw only the petty differences between things, people, and ideologies. If people were to break away from the conventional way of thinking, they would realize the unity of everything, and the pointlessness competing, arguing, or even fighting with one another. Lao-tzu taught rulers to model themselves on the Tao, and Chuang-tzu taught people to become one with it.

T'AI-P'ING CHING (THE SCRIPTURE OF THE ULTIMATE EQUILIBRIUM)

Perhaps because of their cryptic language, both the Tao Te Ching and Chuang-tzu remained philosophical texts rather than religious scriptures until much later, despite the fact that they read very much like mystical texts. The earliest religious Taoist scripture available is T'ai-p'ing Ching. According to Taoist tradition, the deified Lao-tzu inspired a man living in the Eastern Han dynasty called Kan Chi (Gan Ji) to write down this scripture.[4] According to the *History of the Later Han* (Hou-Han Shu), originally the whole scripture contained 170 scrolls, of which only 57 are extant.

Reflected in T'ai-p'ing Ching is the belief in cosmic energies and the correspondence between natural phenomena and human affairs. This scripture identifies three Original Energies known as the Ultimate Yang, the Ultimate Yin, and the Harmonious Neuter. These three energies are expressed in the three Embodied Forms of Heaven, Earth, and human beings, namely fathers, mothers, and children. At first glance, the number three might not appear to correspond well to the dyad of Yin and Yang in the

I-Ching or the Tao Te Ching. Once the interrelations within any threesome are examined, however, one will find that the dual system of Yin and Yang was not at all subverted in the T'ai-p'ing Ching. The sets of three are parallel to one another, which suggests a correspondence between the sets. Just as children are born because their father and mother were joined, the Harmonious Neuter is formed as a consequence of the interaction between the Ultimate Yang and the Ultimate Yin, and humans are generated through the intercourse of the energy of Heaven with the energy of Earth.

This belief in the correspondence between nature and humans leads to an attitude of respect and appreciation toward nature. Chinese people have always been taught to revere and appreciate the origin of their lives, that is, their parents and their ancestors. Since Heaven and Earth (the compound in Chinese is often understood as referring to nature in general) are the parents of human beings, much reverence and gratitude should be paid to them. The belief in a correspondence between nature and humanity further points the way to the "ultimate equilibrium." Just as the Harmonious Neuter is formed through the interaction and balance of the Ultimate Yin and the Ultimate Yang, the harmony and prosperity of human life depend on the interaction and balance of different forces.

TAO-TSANG (TAOIST CANON)

After the T'ai-p'ing Ching appeared during the middle of the Han dynasty, thousands of Taoist scriptures were produced over the ensuing several hundred years. Some of the scriptures continued the T'ai-p'ing Ching's focus on the relationship between humanity and nature, while other texts contained a theoretical mixture of Confucianism, philosophical Taoism, and Yin-Yang and the Five-Element theories, which are discussed in chapter 9. Still other scriptures were liturgical and used in various kinds of rituals, such as rituals to dispel disease and bring long life, and rituals entailing offerings to ancestors and the "parents" of humans, namely, Heaven and Earth.

Among all the rulers from the Eastern Han to the T'ang dynasties, the imperial family of the T'ang dynasty was the strongest supporter of Taoism, though not entirely for religious reasons (as you will see in chapter 9). Among all of the emperors of the T'ang dynasty, the *Emperor Hsüan* (Xuan) of T'ang (c. 712–756 C.E.) was perhaps the most pious. During his reign, he ordered his court officials to collect Taoist scriptures from everywhere throughout the T'ang territory and compile the first Taoist Canon (Tao-tsang). In 748 C.E., the compilation was completed and publicized. Later it was destroyed in the turbulent and war-filled period following the end of the T'ang dynasty.

There were six other attempts to compile Taoist scriptures into a canon: three in the Sung (Song) dynasty (960–1279 C.E.), one in the Chin (Jin) dynasty (1115–1234 C.E.), one in the Yüan (Yuan) dynasty (1279–1368 C.E.), and one in the Ming dynasty (1368–1644 C.E.). The scriptures contained in these compilations ranged from 3,700 scrolls to 7,800 scrolls. Five of these seven compilations were burned or lost in wars, and only two have survived to the present day, namely, the compilations from the Sung and Ming dynasties.

The growth of Taoism, both in terms of scriptures and in terms of religious organizations, had an impact on the growth of Buddhism in China. When Buddhist scriptures were translated into Chinese during the second century C.E., the language of the Tao Te Ching and the Chuang-tzu was borrowed to explain Buddhist ideas; later, when Taoist scriptures were proliferating, Buddhist ideas and terms were borrowed in turn to develop Taoist theories and liturgies. For a very long time, these two religions influenced and competed with each another. The Taoist Canon was compiled partly to make Taoism appear as systematic as Buddhism, which had organized its scriptures into the Three Baskets (tripitaka). Consequently, the scriptures in Tao-tsang were also divided into three branches called the Three Caves (San Tung/San Dong).

4

Worldview

The great Tao flows everywhere.
It may go left or right.
All things depend on it for life,
and it does not turn away from them.
It accomplishes its task, but does not claim credit for it.
It clothes and feeds all things
but does not claim to be master over them.

—Tao Te Ching, Chapter 34

As mentioned in chapter 1, the Chinese character "Tao" means way or road, from which derive the meanings of direction, rule, and principle. The operating principle of the universe is understood to be circularity and balance; therefore, human beings need to attune themselves with Tao in the same manner. Taoists believe there is a correspondence between the universe on the one hand, and human physiology and social life on the other. The human body and human relations originate from nature, so they should be modeled after their origin. "To be one with Tao" therefore means to make one's life correspond to the way things are in the universe and to embody Tao in daily life. Taoist belief in the correspondence between nature and humanity is further evident in the many practical applications of the Yin-Yang and the Five-Element theories, which will be described in this chapter. Applied to time, the Yin-Yang and the Five-Element theories are the foundation of the Chinese Zodiac and the *kan-chih* (Ganzhi) cycle of the Chinese calendar (please refer to chapter 6 and its sidebar); applied to human social life, they are the five relationships; applied to the human body, they are the foundation for Ch'i-kung (Qigong) and Chinese medicine (see chapter 10).

TAO AND ITS MOVEMENT

The word "Tao" is used widely throughout Chinese history. Every philosophical school has its own unique understanding of the operating principle of the universe and the ideal way for human beings to live. In the Tao Te Ching, the word Tao is used to refer to the ultimate reality, the origin of all there is, the Force that keeps the world spinning, the universal truth, and the ideal for which human beings should strive. Tao is maternal in relation to all other things in the world: It nurtures and lets people be themselves. The most readily observable and central characteristic of Tao is its circularity: Night and day succeed each other, and the four seasons follow one after the other. Chapter 25 of the Tao Te Ching says:

> There is a thing confusedly formed, born before heaven and earth. Silent and void, it stands alone and does not change,

> goes round and does not weary. It is capable of being the mother of the world. I know not its name, so I style it "the way." I give it the makeshift name of "the great." Being great, it is further described as receding. Receding, it is described as far away. Being far away, it is described as turning back.[5]

In Chuang-tzu, Tao is described in the following words:

> It is based in itself, rooted in itself. Before heaven and earth came into being, Tao existed by itself from all time. It gave spirits and rulers their spiritual powers. It created heaven and earth. It is above the zenith but it is not high. It is beneath the nadir but it is not low. It is prior to heaven and earth but it is not old. It is more ancient than the highest antiquity but is not regarded as long ago.[6]

Tao is the great origin of the cosmos and the way of the cosmos. It generated and continues to generate everything. It is not a creator, as opposed to the created world; instead, it is a principle that constantly manifests itself in everything it generates. It is conceptually distant and difficult to grasp, and yet it is readily accessible through all phenomena in the world.

Although Tao is in all and encompasses all, it does not impose itself on anything. In chapter 9 of the Tao Te Ching, it is written that Tao is "to retire when the task is accomplished."[7] Tao is not only the "mother" of all things in the world, its "behavior" is quite maternal: "It gives them life and rears them. It gives them life yet claims no possession; it benefits them yet exacts no gratitude; it is the steward yet exercises no authority. Such is called the mysterious virtue."[8] Tao nurtures her children by allowing them to be themselves, so that when they are grown, they will be able to stand on their own. Tao does not demand obedience and does not impose her authority.

The operating principle of the universe is said to be circular; it goes around and does not weary. Tao has generated the myriad of things and is always generating and being present in everything; in other words, it is constantly "working," but it never gets tired. Tao does not get tired because it is self-balancing: After it becomes "great," it recedes, and after it is far away, it returns. This movement of Tao can also be understood in a different way: Tao always gradually moves toward the opposite. Whether understood as self-balancing or as moving toward the opposite, Tao's movement is readily observable in natural phenomena. After it is very hot in the summer, it gradually becomes cold, and the coldness of the winter is replaced by the heat that is returning; the brightest part of the day always gradually recedes to the darkness of the night and vice versa. While the operating principle of the universe is to let everything be, Tao does not allow overgrowth or overdevelopment to go unchecked—whenever something becomes too strong, the opposite arises to maintain balance.

THE MEANING OF VIRTUE (TE/DE)

The Tao Te Ching suggests that a virtuous ruler is a ruler who learns from the movement of Tao and practices Wu-wei, or nonaction. In other words, rulers should model themselves after Tao: As Tao behaves like a mother and lets her children be, rulers are asked to refrain from meddling with people's lives by imposing norms and authorities. Moreover, the idea of Tao manifesting itself in everything paves the way for the belief in the correspondence between what is happening in the universe and what is happening in the human world. Corresponding to Tao's self-balancing movement toward the opposite, the tyrant is destined to be overthrown, and the oppressed will eventually be exalted. This understanding of Tao's self-balancing movement provides guidance to those in positions of political power and brings hope to the oppressed.

As mentioned in chapter 3, both Tao and Te have multiple meanings. Tao is simultaneously the principle of the universe and the ideal toward which people should strive; and Te, virtue, takes shape when one strives to reach that ideal by following the direction of Tao and letting Tao exert its power in human life. In other words, to be virtuous is to be one with Tao and to imitate Tao's movement. Since Tao is always self-balancing, being a virtuous person means to seek a balance in life. One would not like to go to the extreme, since the extreme of something is always accompanied by its opposite. Thus to be respected, one must begin by being humble; for if one is domineering and demanding respect, one is most likely to incur defiance and disobedience. Likewise, in order to establish a state that functions well, a ruler must start by practicing Wu-wei because, knowing that brightness is bound to be balanced by darkness and heat is bound to recede to coldness, an ideal ruler knows it is best to approach a goal by starting from the opposite direction.

Wu-wei does not mean that a ruler should do nothing; neither is it opposed to regulations altogether. Wu-wei only calls for recognition of the role that "nothingness" plays in any practical life. Thirty spokes share one hub. Precisely because therein is "nothing" that you will have the use of the cart. Knead clay in order to make a vessel. Precisely because therein is "nothing" that you will have the use of the vessel. Cut out doors and windows in order to make a room. Precisely because therein is "nothing" that you will have the use of the room.[9]

People usually assume that it is because there are walls that there is a living space but fail to realize that a living space only becomes livable when there is a huge empty space between the walls. In fact, the empty space has to be many times larger than the space occupied by walls. That is, for every "something" (for example, a wall), there has to be much more "nothing" (empty space) to make that something useful. Building too many walls only renders the place uninhabitable. By the same token, imposing too many norms only paralyzes life. The ideal ruler, according to Lao-tzu, knows the usefulness of "nothingness" and knows that a whole lot more can be accomplished by "letting be."

This understanding of Tao and its movement provides the incentive for rulers not to overwhelm the people with power and authority. The same understanding also gives hope to the oppressed and dominated, and justifies their resistance. Since

Tao is in everything, its movement toward the opposite can be observed within everything; this means that any power, if pushed to the extreme, must be subverted.

YIN-YANG AND THE FIVE ELEMENTS

Besides the keen observation of the relation between opposites, which is connected to the Yin-Yang theory, Taoism is also well known for its Five-Element theory. The term "Five Elements" is one of the translations of the Chinese term *Wu-hsing* (Wuxing); it is also translated as Five Forces, Five Agents, Five Phases, and Five Stages. According to Chinese cosmology, in the natural world there are five basic elements: Wood, Fire, Earth, Metal, and Water. Each of the five groups has its Yin and its Yang, corresponding to the Ultimate Yin and the Ultimate Yang. Yin, Yang, and the Five Elements together provide the Chinese people with a framework by which to understand and analyze all phenomena in the world.

Yin and Yang represent any conceptual pair, such as high and low, cold and hot, beautiful and ugly, weak and strong, female and male, life and death. The T'ai-chi succinctly summarizes the relation between the two members of any conceptual pair:

The circle in the top image on page C of the photo insert represents T'ai-chi or the cosmos as a whole. The whole is divided by a curve, with one part being bright and the other being dark. There is a small circle of darkness in the midst of the lighter section and typically a small circle of brightness in the midst of the darker section. The T'ai-chi picture demonstrates that, when something reaches an extreme, the opposite will emerge, and it will emerge not only from the outside but also from the inside. Also, if one draws a straight line going through the center of the circle, dividing the circle into hemispheres, each hemisphere will necessarily contain both brightness and darkness; that is to say, no dichotomy accurately describes the reality. Brightness and darkness form a pair of concepts that may seem entirely incompatible with one another, and yet no moment of the day is completely bright and no moment of the night is completely dark. There is neither pure brightness nor pure darkness, neither pure good nor pure evil, neither pure Yin nor pure Yang. Yin and Yang stand for the two opposites that are contradicting each other and encroaching upon each other, and yet the two are also receding from each other and moving toward each other, supplementing each other, balancing each other, and also containing each other.

Just as Yin and Yang exist in relation to one another, there are positive and negative mutual relations among the Five Elements. The Five Elements work against one another: Wood weakens Earth, Earth weakens Water, Water weakens Fire, Fire weakens Metal, and Metal weakens Wood. They also benefit one another: Wood enhances Fire, Fire enhances Earth, Earth enhances Metal, Metal enhances Water, and Water enhances Wood. The following table is a breakdown of the mutual relations among the Five Elements:

ELEMENT	WEAKENS	ENHANCES	HELPED BY	HARMED BY
Wood	Earth	Fire	Water	Metal
Fire	Metal	Earth	Wood	Water
Earth	Water	Metal	Fire	Wood
Metal	Wood	Water	Earth	Fire
Water	Fire	Wood	Metal	Earth

The "magic number" of five can be found in many aspects of the natural world and human life, such as celestial bodies, colors and tastes, human internal organs, and spatial and temporal categories. The celestial bodies that correspond to Wood, Fire, Earth, Metal, and Water are the five major planets: Jupiter, Mars, Saturn, Venus, and Mercury, respectively. In colors, there are green, red, yellow, white, and black. In tastes, there are sour, bitter, sweet, spicy, and salty. In human internal organs, there are the liver, heart, spleen, lungs, and kidneys.[10] There are five spatial categories, composed of the four directions (north, south, east, and west) and the center. There are also five temporal categories, with a Center in each of the four seasons. For example, the first through third months on the lunar calendar are considered spring, and the second month is the center of the spring.

In many cases, the five categories can be further divided into Yin and Yang. The Yin-Yang and Five-Element theories, applied to time, form the basis of the Chinese Zodiac and the kan-chih cycle (see the sidebar in chapter 6). Applied to space, they are the foundation of feng shui. Applied to the human body, they are the framework of Chinese medical theories and Ch'i-kung (Qigong). Chapters 6 and 10 discuss the applications of the Yin-Yang and Five-Element theories in more detail.

5

Worship:
A Visit to a Taoist Temple

Doors and windows are cut out to make a room,
But it is on its non-being
that the utility of the room depends.
Therefore turn being into advantage
and turn non-being into utility.

—Tao Te Ching, Chapter 11

Religious practice in Taoist temples tends to integrate elements of Chinese folk tradition and other popular rituals. Incense burning and paper money burning, originally closely related to ancestor worship, have now become two of the most common practices among Taoists. Different kinds of incense and paper money are used, depending on which deities are worshipped. Many believers also light candles while they worship. Two other common practices, bamboo root divination and casting divinatory sticks, are used to ask deities for guidance. These last two practices are heavily influenced by the Book of Change (I-Ching) and shaped both by Confucian moral teachings and by the Taoist emphasis on circularity and relativity. As a folk religion, Taoism has generally been very tolerant and accommodating. Taoism's deities have many different origins; some are religious figures from other religions, while other deities are historical figures who have won the reverence and esteem of the populace. The Lung-Shan (Longshan) Temple in Taipei, Taiwan, is a good example of Taoism's tendency to include elements from a variety of religions. It is also a temple in which all of the practices mentioned above can be observed, and the temple can also be accessed on-line at www.lungshan.org.tw/home.htm.

A MELTING POT OF DEITIES

There are three "courts," or areas, in the Lung-Shan Temple: the front court, the center court, and the back court. The front court is somewhat like a public square with vendors selling offerings for the deities. On major holidays, such as the Lantern Festival (see chapter 8), exhibitions and public activities often take place in the front court. The Lung-Shan Temple can easily be mistaken for a Buddhist temple should one look only at the deities worshipped in the center court. Occupying the central space is the Buddhist Bodhisattva Avalokiteśvara (Kuan-yin or Guanyin in Chinese, Kannon in Japanese), the most beloved mother-like deity of the Chinese people. On her left side is the Buddhist Bodhisattva Mañjuśri (Wen-shu/ Wenshu), and on her right side, the Buddhist Bodhisattva Samantabhadra (P'u-hsien/Puxian).

At the left of Mañjuśri is Skanda (Wei-t'o/ Weituo), originally a warrior-god in Hinduism who was later incorporated into Buddhism as a guardian of the Buddhist doctrine. At the right of Samantabhadra is Saṉghārāma (Ch'ieh-lan/Qielan), a guardian of all temples and places for self-cultivation. Scattered among these five Buddhist bodhisattvas and in the background are the "Eighteen Buddhist Saints," called arhants. By Chinese convention a central location indicates importance, thus one might assume that the Lung-Shan Temple is a Buddhist temple, but that would be an incorrect assumption. The largest incense-receiving tripod in the entire temple is dedicated to the Jade Emperor (*Yü-huang shang-ti*/Yuhuang shangdi), a deity who is certainly Taoist, not Buddhist. After stepping into the temple and lighting the incense sticks, the worshipper prays or at least pays homage to the Jade Emperor before worshipping any other deities. In addition, almost all the deities in the back court are distinctly Taoist. In fact, there are a total of 166 deities worshipped in the Lung-Shan Temple, each varying in importance and status, and most of them are uniquely Taoist; in other words, the Lung-Shan Temple is ultimately revealed to be a Taoist temple.

The back court of the Lung-Shan Temple consists of three chambers. In the middle of the central chamber is the Goddess of Birth (Chu-sheng niang-niang/Zhusheng niangniang), with more than a dozen minor deities on her sides assisting with pregnancy and child-raising. Also in the central chamber are the Eminent King of Water Immortals (Shui-hsien tsun-wang/ Shuixian zunwang), the God of Marriage (Yüe-hsia lao-jen/ Yuexia laoren), the Local Earth God (Fu-te cheng-shen/Fude zhengshen, or more popularly called T'u-ti-kung/Tudigong), and the Regional Underworld God (Ch'eng-huang/Chenghuang).

Many scholars identify the Eminent King of Water Immortals as Ta Yü (Da Yu), the founder of the Hsia (Xia) dynasty (2100–1600 B.C.E.), who spent his life solving the flooding problem of the Yellow River and who has been revered for his great contribution to public welfare. The God of Marriage is depicted as a white-haired old man with a reel of red thread in his hands. It is believed that if he ties one end of a thread onto a person and the other end onto another person, then those two people will definitely be married. The Local Earth God is one of the most popular deities and is seen everywhere in Chinese societies. In small home shrines, many believers display a portrait or sculpture of the Local Earth God and his consort. To Chinese people, he is readily accessible, amiable, and closely related to people's daily life. The Regional Underworld God governs the same locality as the Local Earth God, though their roles differ. In the popular understanding, the Local Earth God is in charge of well-being in the living world, while the Regional Underworld God protects people from malicious ghosts, records the merits and demerits of people, and may inflict punishment accordingly after people die.

In Taoist terminology, if one faces the same direction as the central deity, one's left side is called the direction of the green dragon (or simply the dragon side) and one's right side is the direction of the white tiger (or the tiger side). There are usually large numbers of students clustered in front of the chamber on the dragon side in the back court (that is, the chamber at the left hand of the Goddess of Birth) because three deities related to academic advancement are situated there. In the middle is the Star-God of Scholarly Brilliance (Wen-ch'ang hsing-chün/Wenchang xingjun), who is riding the Horse of Wealth. At his left hand is the Star-God of Literary Advancement (Ta-k'uei hsing-chün/Dakui xingjun). This term refers to the first star of the Big Dipper, which is associated with high scholarly status in Taoist astrology. At the right hand of the Star-God of Scholarly Brilliance is the Venerable Scholar Tzu-yang (Ziyang). Tzu-yang is another name for Chu Hsi (Zhu Xi) (1130–1200 C.E.), a famous Confucian scholar in the Southern Sung (Song) dynasty (1127–1279 C.E.) who established the standardized Confucian curriculum.

Sitting in the middle of the chamber on the tiger side (that is, the chamber at the right hand of the Goddess of Birth) is the Sage Emperor Kuan (Guan). He was a historical figure named Kuan

Yü (Guan Yu) who lived from 221 to 263 C.E. during the Three Kingdoms period (220–280 C.E.). Though he was called the "sage emperor," he was not an "emperor" and he never desired to be one; the word "emperor" was simply added to his title to denote people's great respect for him. Kuan Yü has been known and revered primarily because of his unwavering loyalty to his emperor, whom he also recognized as his older brother. Kuan Yü was the most prominent warrior in Chinese history because he not only displayed his prowess by fighting and leading the army, but he was also an extraordinarily courageous man, well-educated, and possessed a great talent for business. People worship him for different reasons: to have a better relationship with one's siblings or colleagues, to establish social responsibility and group loyalty, to dispel one's fear and be brave, to be nimble in physical movements or to improve one's health, and to succeed in business. At his sides are the Emperors of the Three Realms (San-kuan ta-ti/Sanguan dadi; also called San-chieh kung or Sanjiegong in some regions) and the Kşitigarbha Bodhisattva (Ti-tsang/Dizang; Jizo in Japanese). The Emperors of the Three Realms are respected as the sovereigns who govern and protect the heavenly realm, the earthly realm, and the watery realm. Kşitigarbha Bodhisattva voluntarily entered Hell and swore that he would indefinitely postpone his achievement of Buddhahood until all of the miserable beings in Hell were lifted out of their depravity. The Emperors of the Three Realms are obviously Taoist, while the Kşitigarbha Bodhisattva is clearly of Buddhist origin. Here again we see the tendency of Taoism to include elements from various religions and origins: Religious figures from both Taoism and Buddhism are placed alongside a historical figure, and yet believers do not see anything wrong with that. In a side extension of this chamber, there is another historical figure named the Immortal Master Hua-t'o (Huatuo). A contemporary of Kuan Yü, Hua-t'o was worshipped because he was a doctor who had unfathomable knowledge about medicine and could cure every disease and repair every injury.

A PILGRIM'S PATH THROUGH THE TEMPLE

The main gates of the Lung-Shan Temple are rarely open except for major holidays (see chapter 8), so worshippers usually enter the temple through a smaller gate on the dragon side, called the Dragon Gate, and leave through the Tiger Gate. One can either purchase incense sticks from one of the vendors in the side chambers near the Dragon Gate or take those provided by the temple, for which the worshipper usually puts some money in the donation box. Along with incense sticks, one may also want to buy at least three kinds of snacks or fruit, paper money, and candles. Worshippers then place the snacks or fruits on a plate and put the plate, together with the paper money, on one of the tables as offerings. There are several pairs of candle-holding racks between the main gates and the incense-receiving tripod dedicated to the Jade Emperor. If one wishes to light candles, one would usually light a pair of candles and place them on the racks, one on the left and one on the right, before lighting the incense sticks. Sometimes candles are lit simply to honor the deities, but more often people are lighting them to pray for a bright future, a long life, or both. Next, one lights the incense sticks, faces the main gates and the incense-receiving tripod, holds the incense in front of one's forehead, and starts to pray. An example of a typical prayer would be:

> Jade Emperor, today your devotee ___________ (one's own name), who lives at ___________ (one's address), comes to the Lung-Shan Temple to pay homage to Your Majesty. Your devotee has humbly lit a pair of candles and prepared a few foods in dedication to you, and I would be most grateful if Your Majesty could kindly grant safety and good health (or longevity, or other things the worshipper would like).

The paper money is usually not mentioned in the prayer, just as when a Chinese person provides compensation to someone respected (such as a teacher, a skillful artist, or a professional Taoist), it is not offered publicly nor is it recognized as a payment. People, grateful for the kindly assistance they have received, conventionally put the compensation in a red envelope and hide it where the receiver will find it. This ritualizes the idea that those people who are respected and of a higher social status cannot be bought; they are providing their special knowledge or skills because they are kind or compassionate, not because they want to be paid. After praying, the worshipper puts three sticks in the tripod and then goes over to the central court.

To pray to the bodhisattvas in the central court, one needs to climb a few stairs because the central court is above ground level. Since the Avalokiteśvara Bodhisattva is exceedingly compassionate and cares deeply for all beings, people usually pray longer here. If believers are suffering from any sort of discomfort or pain, whether a debilitating disease, financial crisis, relationship problems, or just a general sense of disorientation, they will report the sufferings to the bodhisattva in detail and pray for protection or guidance. Even if believers do not have a significant problem at the moment, they may still pray longer here, hoping to procure more blessings. Then the worshipper will put another three incense sticks into the tripod located immediately in front of Avalokiteśvara. Although there are other bodhisattvas in the central court who are just as important in Buddhism, Taoists focus on Avalokiteśvara, only mentioning the others' names and titles in passing. They then proceed to spend considerably more time in the back court worshipping or praying to those deities whose identities are clearly Taoist. This fact again demonstrates that the Lung-Shan Temple is primarily a Taoist temple, even though the Buddhist bodhisattvas are at the center and are situated above other deities.

In the back court stands a separate row of tables for the offerings dedicated to the deities there, as well as five incense-receiving tripods of various sizes. Three of the tripods are in front of the central chamber; the largest of these is dedicated to the deity in the middle, the Goddess of Birth. The other two tripods in front of the central chamber are the same size. There are two candle-holding racks here, too, and if worshipers are praying for a bright future with a happy family, they may want to light candles and dedicate them to the Goddess of Birth and her assistants. A separate pair of candle-holding racks and an incense-receiving tripod are placed in front of the chamber on the dragon side and another pair in front of the chamber on the tiger side. The tripods for these two side chambers are slightly larger than the smaller ones in front of the central chamber but not as large as the one in the middle chamber. As we have already mentioned, the dragon side of the chamber houses three deities associated with scholarly work and academic progress. Many students and their worried parents come to the Lung-Shan Temple primarily to seek blessings from these three deities. Since candles symbolize a bright future, believers would dedicate a pair of candles to these three deities, praying for a bright academic future. The candle-holding racks in front of this chamber are usually much more crowded than the other racks in the back court.

If people buy a small pack of twelve incense sticks from the vendors, they would put one incense stick in each of the five tripods in the back court, three of them at the tripod dedicated to the Jade Emperor, and another three to the bodhisattvas in the center court. There will be one left, and worshippers will go back to the front and pay homage to the Jade Emperor once again. With a medium pack of eighteen incense sticks, three are placed in each of the three larger tripods in the back court and one in each of the two smaller tripods; then the worshippers will go back to the Jade Emperor with the remaining one as well. A large pack has twenty-four sticks, and the believers will simply put three in all seven tripods in the temple and then return to the front with three sticks. There are two reasons for going back to the front court. First, the Jade Emperor is recognized as the sovereign of all sovereigns, so extra respect is shown by praying to him twice; second, the Taoist worldview emphasizes circularity. Returning again to the Jade Emperor is a way of literally bringing things full circle by returning to where the believer began.

There are many kinds of paper money. Some are fine and smooth on the surface, while others are coarse and thick; some are about fifteen inches square, others are approximately six inches square, and still others are about 3-by-3 ½ inches. There is usually a shiny piece of paper on the top but some are red in color, others are gold, and still others are silver. When the top piece is red, some have drawings of ancient state officials, yet others are plain. If one is dedicating the paper money to the deities associated with sovereignty, such as those with "emperor" in their titles, the large finer paper money with drawings on the red top piece is used. If, on the other hand, the paper money is for one's own ancestors, the small coarse kind with a plain silver top piece is used. If believers worship at home, they will burn the paper money in a metal bucket at their own front door. Some have two metal buckets, one for deities and the other for ancestors. Some people even have separate buckets for major and minor deities. In the Lung-Shan Temple, all different kinds of paper money are burned in the same "Money Booth" at the tiger side of the temple. This is for the sake of safety; it is easier to watch and care for one fire instead of three.

SEEKING GUIDANCE

A believer who wants guidance from the deities on a particular question may engage in bamboo root divination. A bamboo root is cut in the middle to form a pair of "cups" (although nowadays those cups are usually not made of bamboo). The worshipper holds the pair of cups in front of his forehead, asks a particular deity a question that can be answered simply with a yes or no, bows three times, and then throws the cups into the air. If one of the cups lands on the inner side and the other on the outer side, the inquirer has "the sacred cups" or "the golden cups" and the answer is yes. If the result is "the smiling cups," with both cups showing the inner side, it means that the question was not asked in an appropriate manner (perhaps not in a way that can be answered by a yes or no reply) or that for some reason the answer has to be withheld from the inquirer.

If both cups are showing the outer side, the inquirer has "the negative cups" and the answer is no. This kind of divination is based on the combination of Yin and Yang, which is the foundation of the I-Ching (see chapter 3 for more about the I-Ching). In the spirit of Taoism, rather than having two Yins or two Yangs, it is better to have both and thereby have a balance. Many believers have these kinds of cups in the mini-shrine at their home to answer their daily questions, and some people would use two coins if they needed to ask a yes-no question but did not have a formal pair of cups. Usually the question asked is not something as important as "Should I marry this person?" Instead, the question is something like "Shall I burn the paper money right now?" After one finishes praying and has placed the incense sticks in the incense-receiver, it is customary to wait for at least a half-hour before burning the paper money so that the deities have time to enjoy the offerings.

If one seeks a more detailed answer, one can cast the divinatory sticks. The sticks are numbered, usually from one to sixty-four, because in the Book of Change there are a total of sixty-four combinations made by combining any two of the Eight Trigrams (pa-kua/bagua). The Eight Trigrams are in turn constructed from the Yin and Yang symbols (see chapter 6 for more about the Chinese trigrams). The sticks are placed in a cylinder-shaped holder, and the inquirer, after asking the question, shakes the holder until one of the sticks suddenly jumps up. Next, the inquirer goes to the drawers in which divinatory poems are placed and finds the poem with the same number as the stick that jumped up. Some of the poems carry Confucian moral teachings, others denote the Taoist notions of circularity and relativity, and still others are simply obscure. The divinatory poems may or may not be readily applicable to the situation in question, so the inquirer may need to seek the assistance of the professional Taoists in order to understand the poem's relevance to his or her question.

6

Growing Up Taoist

Prepare for the difficult while it is still easy.
Deal with the big while it is still small.
Difficult undertakings have always
started with what is easy,
And great understandings have always
started with what is small.
Therefore the sage never strives for the great,
And thereby the great is achieved.

—Tao Te Ching, Chapter 63

Though most Chinese people do not identify themselves exclusively as Taoists, much of their lives are influenced by a Taoist worldview embodied in beliefs and practices like the Chinese Zodiac and feng shui. On the popular level, as we have seen, the Three Teachings (Confucianism, Buddhism, and Taoism) are not completely distinguishable from one another. For example, Taoist sensibilities regarding ancestor worship are shared by Confucianism, and Taoist funeral rituals are often mingled with Buddhist rites. Of course, there is still a group of Taoist practitioners who identify themselves more exclusively as Taoist and more consciously abide by Taoist beliefs and regulations; these may be lay people who identify themselves as Taoists or may be professional Taoists called Tao-shih (Daoshi). The basic practices commonly carried out by Taoists of various schools include the cultivation of Ch'i (Qi), vegetarianism, and morning and evening scripture recitation.

THE CHINESE ZODIAC

Many Americans come to know about the twelve animals of the Chinese Zodiac through their dining experiences in Chinese restaurants. As a way of attracting American customers, many Chinese restaurants have paper placemats printed with brief descriptions of the Chinese Zodiac. People who travel to such places as China, Taiwan, and Hong Kong are often disappointed to find that most restaurants there do not have Chinese Zodiac placemats; but that does not mean that Chinese people do not know or care about their animal signs. Even though the Chinese Zodiac is often publicly denounced as superstition, practically every Chinese person knows her or his animal sign. There is a sequence of twelve animal signs that repeats in the same order,[11] so that each animal sign recurs every twelve years. This makes it relatively easy to deduce a person's age if you know his or her animal sign. (The correct way to find out a person's animal sign is to ask which animal he or she belongs to.) For example, if someone born in 1980 (the year of the Monkey) sees a person who looks about his age or maybe a few years older, and after inquiry finds out the latter was born in the year of the Serpent, which corresponds to 1977, then the former knows for certain that the latter is three years older than himself.

The Chinese Zodiac also affects people's actions and interactions in other ways. Birth rates rise noticeably in the Year of the Dragon, because to Chinese people the dragon symbolizes freedom, power, fortune, and high social status. When the year is in the sign in which they were born, those individuals visit Taoist temples to ask professional Taoists to perform rituals to ensure their safety and cure their ailments because it is believed that life is more difficult for people during their animal year. The twelve animals are associated with different personality traits, and some animal signs are considered compatible (or incompatible) with each other. In general, it is believed that people of certain animal signs, such as the Rabbit and the Rooster, easily get into conflict with each other. If a Rabbit and a Rooster fall in love and want

THE KAN-CHIH (GANZHI) CYCLE OF THE CHINESE CALENDAR

The Kan-chih cycle was formed by combining two sets of counters, the ten "heavenly stems" (t'ien-kan/tiangan) and the twelve "earthly branches" (ti-chih/dizhi). The ten stems have the nature of *Yang* Wood, *Yin* Wood, *Yang* Fire, *Yin* Fire, *Yang* Earth, *Yin* Earth, *Yang* Metal, *Yin* Metal, *Yang* Water, and *Yin* Water, respectively. The twelve branches correspond to the twelve animal signs in the Chinese Zodiac. In the Chinese Zodiac, each year is given an animal's name; thus, the year 1961 is the year of the ox, while 1962 is the year of the tiger. The ten stems and twelve branches are combined to form sixty combinations that have been used to count the years throughout Chinese history. After sixty years, the Chinese calendar returns to the exact same stem and branch combination. The Chinese call the first of these sixty combinations chia-tzu (jiazi); this name is formed by combining the term chia (jia), meaning the first stem, and tzu (zi), meaning the first branch. The term chia-tzu also refers to a sixty-year time span. Sometimes older Chinese people say, "I have lived for one chia-tzu" instead of "I have lived for sixty years."

to get married, they might be discouraged by their parents or friends who take traditional beliefs seriously, because theoretically their relationship should not be a happy one. It is also believed that people of certain animal signs, such as the Rat and the Ox, tend to get along and become good friends.

FENG SHUI

The practice of feng shui is based on the Yin-Yang and Five-Element theories. Feng shui is also rooted in the Taoists' appreciation for nature and their concern for maintaining harmony between humanity and nature. Indispensable in feng shui practice is the octagon formed by the Eight Trigrams, which is Taoist is origin. Since Taoist philosophy has become an integral part of Chinese culture, many Chinese practice feng shui without realizing its Taoist roots.

The most basic framework of feng shui practice is the division of space into five categories in association with the Five Elements. The East is associated with the Wood element, the South with the Fire element, the West with the Metal element, the North with the Water element, and the Center with the Earth element. As the Five Elements are associated with five colors, the five geographical categories have their colors, too: the East is green, the South is red, the West is white (or a silvery color), the North is black, and the Center is yellow. The Taoist worldview suggests that the cosmos is in constant change, with different forces enhancing or diminishing one another (see the table in chapter 4 for the relations among the Five Elements). At each moment there is a unique relation among the Five Elements, and one or more forces may be stronger while others are weakened. Since Taoist worldview also suggests that there is a profound correlation between what is happening in the cosmos and what is happening in the human world, it is believed that the particular balance or imbalance of the Five Elements at the moment of one's birth is reflected in one's body and affects one's life. If one's life is deficient in the Fire element, one may want to direct the energy of nature to the South side of her room by placing a crystal ball or hanging a wind chime there. She may also be encouraged to wear red (Fire) and green (Wood), since Wood enhances Fire. Moving to the North may negatively affect the course of this person's life, for the North is associated with Water, and Water works against Fire. A person may even be given a name with the Chinese characters that contains the character for Fire.

Feng shui is also closely connected to Yin-Yang theory. As stated in chapter 3, each of the Eight Trigrams is composed of three symbols, some combination of Yin and Yang. In the octagon of the Eight Trigrams, the space is further divided into eight directions (and a center). Each direction is associated with an aspect of human life, in addition to having its own color. The Southwest, for example, is associated with pink and relationships or marriage, and the Northeast with blue and knowledge or self-cultivation. A professional Taoist (Tao-shih) might recommend that a couple with marital problems move their master bedroom to the southwest side of the house and decorate the room with pink. The Tao-shih may also give more detailed instructions based on the person's gender, because the goal of feng shui practice is to reach a balance of the Five Elements as well as a balance of the Yin and the Yang.

LIFE AND DEATH IN TAOISM

Taoism values life from its inception. The Taoist appreciation of life is not only reflected in its quest for longevity and the protection of life but also in the respect paid to the origin of life. Because of a common attitude of gratitude toward the origin of one's life, Taoism and Confucianism share the spiritual practices of filial piety and ancestor worship. Due to concern for the afterlife of parents and ancestors, complicated funeral rituals have been developed. The beliefs and practices of Taoism and Buddhism converge so well in this regard that quite often in Chinese funerals both Tao-shih and Buddhist monks and nuns are present, and both Taoist and Buddhist liturgies and scriptures are recited.

Taoism and Confucianism similarly teach people to respect and to be grateful for their own origin, though the scope and emphasis of their concerns are not exactly the same. Confucianism is primarily concerned with the most immediate origin of one's life, namely, one's parents, and therefore stresses filial piety. Taoism teaches filial piety, too, and yet, because in Taoism the origin of human beings is traced back to the Ultimate Yin and Ultimate Yang of the cosmos (see chapter 3), Taoism demands appreciation and gratitude toward all of nature as well as filial piety. The spiritual practice common to both Taoism and Confucianism is ancestor worship. Filial piety and ancestor worship are actually two sides of the same coin: If one should display gratitude toward ancestors, considering that parents are the closest ancestors, one should display gratitude toward parents as well. From another viewpoint, if one should revere parents as the people who gave life to oneself, considering that ancestors are one's parents from generations in the past, ancestors must surely be revered.

When a person dies, the children or other close relatives typically hire a Tao-shih, or a Buddhist monk, or both, to perform funeral rituals, hoping to reduce the misery the deceased might experience in the afterlife. One of the biggest concerns is that the deceased will suffer because of misdeeds performed in life. The suffering is conceptualized in the form of being lost and stuck somewhere in the underworld forever, in the form of punishments in the hells, or in the form of revenge by the spirits of the victims of this person's misdeeds. It is believed that the spirit of the deceased needs to cross an exceedingly dark river in order to cross over to the Land of Darkness, where other spirits and Hell Judges dwell. Therefore, the professional funeral ritual performers (usually more than one) typically light candles to illuminate the way for the deceased. In some regions where there is a river or a lake nearby, people might also fold paper into the shape of a boat or a lotus, place a candle on it, and let it float down the river or into the center of the lake. Believing that the deceased might be judged and punished in many layers of hells, Taoist and Buddhist scriptures and liturgies are recited to seek pardon from the Hell Judges, as well as to pray for help from some mighty beings, including the Buddhas and bodhisattvas of Buddhism. It is believed that children may repent on behalf of their deceased parents and thereby reduce the severity of the punishments the deceased parents might be receiving. A feast is provided for the beings in the Land of Darkness with the hope that those who might want to seek revenge would leave the recently deceased alone. Sometimes, if financial resources allow, the children might make offerings to all of the beings in the Three Realms, including deities, hoping that the deities would protect the deceased parent from harassment by beings in the Land of Darkness. By the same token, various types of paper money used by the beings in the Three Realms are burned, either to seek protection from the deities or to appease revenge-seeking spirits.

SELF-CULTIVATION OF PROFESSIONAL TAOISTS

Taoism affects many aspects of Chinese life without people being aware of the Taoist origins of many of their beliefs and customs. There is also a group of people who are conscious of Taoist roots and are serious about following the teachings of Lao-tzu, Chuang-tzu, Chang Tao-ling, and other eminent Taoist masters. Typically these worshippers engage in practices to cultivate their life force, or Ch'i (Qi), refrain from eating animal products, and read Taoist scriptures twice a day.

People who deliberately and consciously identify themselves as Taoists devote considerable time to the cultivation of Ch'i. The cultivation of Ch'i starts with regulating one's own breathing, since the life force can hardly be concentrated or purified when one is short of breath. There are some techniques for the gathering of the positive energy in the universe, but these special techniques are transmitted from masters to disciples and thus not known to outsiders. A Ch'i cultivator also needs to have some knowledge about Chinese medical theory, since one has to know the relations among one's internal organs in order to know where or through what route one should direct the positive energy. The cultivation of Ch'i serves at least two purposes: one is for physical health, longevity, and hopefully immortality, and the other is to be in tune with the energy of nature and to grasp the true meaning and movement of Tao.

One requirement for the cultivation of Ch'i is the ability to concentrate. When one is too attached to artificial tastes, it is very difficult to concentrate; therefore Taoist practitioners prefer vegetables and fruits because they have natural and simple flavors. Taoists refrain from eating animal products in part out of Taoist respect for all life and partly out of self-interest. From its beginnings, Taoism has been preoccupied with the respect for and preservation of life (as in the Chuang-tzu; see chapters 2 and 3), and Tao has been conceptualized as a mother who nurtures the myriad of things in the universe and lets them be themselves (as in the Tao Te Ching; see chapter 3). For these reasons, Taoists are expected to refrain from imposing their wills on others through violence. Killing other beings in order to eat is a highly questionable thing to do because Tao is the nurturer rather than destroyer of lives. Doing something that is in direct conflict with Tao is not desirable. Destroying lives for food may drag people down and away from Tao; in this regard, Taoists practice vegetarianism out of self-interest.

Besides Ch'i cultivation and vegetarianism, Taoist practitioners also sit still and recite scriptures twice a day. These are called the morning and evening lessons, and they are performed for the purposes of enhancing health and attuning oneself to the Tao. The morning lesson is recited from 5 A.M. to 7 A.M. When one first awakes after a night's sleep, the Ch'i in one's body is predominantly the Yin, and the Yang is just about to rise. Sitting down and concentrating on scripture recitation is said to bring the two forces into balance and to bring peace physically and mentally to the practitioner for the day. From 5 P.M. to 7 P.M., one is tired and stressed, while the Yang is declining and the Yin growing. Reciting the evening lesson at this time can release the stress and restore one's energy. The scriptures used for the morning and evening lessons may deal with the concept of Tao. Taoist practitioners also recite texts that praise the merits of the founders of their schools (denominations) as well as texts replete with moral injunctions. The recitation makes the Taoist want to follow in the footsteps of the Taoist founders, to understand the true meaning of Tao, and to be one with Tao by being moral.

Taoist practices and the applications of Taoist thought to life are discussed further in chapters 8 and 10.

7

Cultural Expressions

Tao is empty like a bowl,
It may be used but its capacity is never exhausted.
It is bottomless, perhaps the ancestor of all things.
It blunts its sharpness,
It unties its tangles.
It becomes one with the dusty world.

—Tao Te Ching, Chapter 4

The visitor to the Chinese cultural realm will have no trouble finding artifacts that illustrate Taoist concepts, paintings and sculptures of Taoist deities, Taoist talismans, and popular literature that preaches Taoist doctrines, but Taoist cultural expressions are not limited to those that can be clearly identified as Taoist. During the Eastern Chin (Jin) dynasty (317–420 C.E.), Taoism won the favor of many aristocrats. During this same time period, it absorbed elements from Buddhism, which was far more systematic than Taoism was at that time. Ever since then, the spirit of Taoism can be seen in literature and art created both by those who identify themselves as Taoists and those who do not. Many Chinese poems express a typically Taoist appreciation of nature, and most Chinese landscape paintings reflect a Taoist understanding of the relationship between humans and nature. The flow of Ch'i (Qi; frequently translated as cosmic energies or life forces) is perhaps the most emphasized aspect of Chinese calligraphy. Taoist architecture has evolved together with the Chinese building tradition, and both emphasize the Taoist approach of becoming one with the natural environment. Taoist music has been patronized by emperors of many different dynasties, and yet paradoxically it often blends with local folk music and carries regional characteristics. As a religion indigenous to China, Taoism has truly pervaded and permeated many aspects of Chinese culture.

FUNCTIONAL ARTS

Taoism contains many different schemes for categorizing the phenomena in the world, for example, Yin and Yang, the Five Elements, and the twelve earthly branches (see the sidebar in chapter 6). The different schemes may have come from different traditions and are not always easily understood; moreover, they can make Taoism appear unsystematic and inconsistent. Consequently, Taoist arts are often dedicated to the systematic illustration of Taoist concepts. The Diagram of the Supreme Ultimate, for instance, is an illustration of the oppositional yet complementary and mutually explanatory relation between Yin and Yang, as well as their unity within Tao. Prior to the emergence of this T'ai-chi (Taiji) diagram, the Yin and the Yang were symbolized by a tiger and a dragon (or, alternatively, a turtle and a crane, especially in Japanese art); the new T'ai-chi diagram expresses the oppositional yet complementary relationship between Yin and Yang better than the animal comparisons.

Another form of Taoist art is the writing or drawing of talismans. The words and drawings on Taoist talismans are supposed to contain the fundamental energies of the cosmos and thus have the power to transform reality. After professional Taoists say prayers, they burn the talismans and put the ashes in warm water. There are believers who drink the water with the talisman ashes in order to tap into the cosmic energies to cure their diseases, protect themselves from negative forces that are lurking, rejuvenate their relationships with their loved ones, and so on. More serious practitioners also meditate after consuming the talismans so that they can fully absorb the essences of the magical powers contained in them. In some talismans, the Chinese characters are totally separate from the drawings, while in others some of the strokes of the characters are extended to form part of the drawings. The talisman writer or artist usually finishes the entire drawing in one breath, and the words and drawings are often symmetrical. Talisman writing has become an important branch of Chinese calligraphy.

THE AWESOMENESS OF NATURE

Many famous and respected poets and painters throughout Chinese history were closely associated with Taoism. One of the major themes in their works is the awesomeness of nature and, simultaneously, the pleasure of being one with nature. Hsieh Ling-Yün (Xie Lingyun; 385–433 C.E.), a famous landscape poet living in the Eastern Chin dynasty, when the Tao was diligently pursued by aristocrats, is highly praised for his exquisite descriptions of the beauty of the mountains, lakes, and rivers. Many people are familiar with Li Po (Li Bo; 701–762 C.E.), a great poet who lived during the T'ang dynasty. Li Po expressed his great love for nature and his enjoyment of being in the natural environment:

> You ask me why I dwell in mountains green?
> I smile and don't reply; my heart feels just at peace.
> Peace blossoms with the stream float far away . . .
> This is another world, not that of humans.[12]

Li Po is commonly honored as the "Immortal of Poetry" because his words flow so naturally and his imagination is beyond limit. Since reaching immortality is the highest ideal for most Taoist practitioners, the title "immortal" also indicates his religious affiliation with Taoism. Li Po was also designated a "True Person of Highest Purity" (Shang-ch'ing chen-jen/ Shangqing zhenren), which shows that he was well respected by Taoists, because "highest purity" (shang-ch'ing/shangqing) is the honorary title of one of the three highest deities in Taoism.

Among the outstanding painters associated with Taoism is Ku K'ai-chih (Gu Kaizhi; c. 345–406 C.E.), one of the greatest painters of the Eastern Chin dynasty. He was renowned for his vivid portraits and landscapes. The character "chih" (zhi) in his name showed his affiliation with the Way of the Heavenly Master (*T'ien-shih Tao*/Tianshi Dao). Wu Tao-tzu (Wu Daozi; active c. 710–760), a court painter of the T'ang dynasty, was honored as the "Saint of Painting." He was particularly famous for his landscape paintings and his drawings of Lao-tzu and other Taoist deities. Allegedly, many people converted to Taoism upon seeing his drawings of the deities; and Taoist liturgical painters of later times tried to imitate him because his paintings were so remarkable. Another landscape painter was Chü-jan (Juran; active c. 960–980 C.E.), a court painter in the Northern Sung (Song) dynasty. Although Chü-jan was a Buddhist monk, his landscape painting entitled "Seeking the Tao in the Autumn Mountains" vividly conveys Taoist ideas and is similar to the painting titled "Through the Autumn Mountains with a Lute in Hand" on page H of the photo insert. The Tao can be sought in the natural environment because the cosmic process that created the terrestrial landscape is also the spiritual life force that forms human beings. The path that is leading into and consumed by the mountains symbolizes the Tao—both the difficulty of searching for it and the rarity of finding it. The proportion of human beings (the recluse and his guest) to nature (the mountains) signifies the nonanthropocentric worldview and the Taoist ideal of being at one with nature.

THE FLOW OF CH'I

The Taoist emphasis on the flow of Ch'i is most significantly reflected in Chinese calligraphy. The calligraphy of Wang Hsi-chih (Wang Xizhi; 307–365 C.E.; alternative dates 321–379), who is called the "Saint of Calligraphy," is recognized by Chinese people as the greatest of all time precisely because of the smooth transitions between different strokes. In Taoist terms, this smooth transition between the strokes depicts the flow of the Ch'i. A nephew of the first prime minister of the Eastern Chin dynasty, Wang Hsi-chih was a practicing Taoist, like many of the aristocrats of his time. The character "chih" in his name, as in that of Ku K'ai-chih (see the previous section), was an indication of his family's adherence to the Way of the Heavenly Master. According to the *Chin Shu* (*Jinshu*), the standard history of the Chin dynasty, Wang Hsi-chih was very serious about Taoist practices and would gather special herbs and minerals that were supposed to bring about a healthy, long life.

Famous calligraphers are generally known for their expertise in a certain style of calligraphy, but Wang Hsi-chih was a master in many styles. For example, he was accomplished in the formal style (k'ai-shu/kaishu), the running style (hsing-shu/xingshu), and the cursive style (ts'ao-shu/caoshu); however, he is most admired for his hsing-ts'ao style, which is halfway between the running and the cursive styles. The most exquisite demonstration of his hsing-ts'ao style is the "Preface to the Anthology of the Orchid Pavilion" (Lan-t'ing-chi hsü/Lantingjixu). His most important work, however, is his "Scripture of the Yellow Court"

(Huang-t'ing Ching/Huangting jing), composed in the formal style. This scripture is significant because it describes the concept of Inner Alchemy (nei-tan/neidan) in early Taoism and the method for practicing it. According to the Taoist theory of correspondence between humanity and nature, the human body is compared to a terrestrial landscape in some schools or to the entire cosmos in others. Different parts of the body are inhabited by different deities, just as different regions of the cosmos are inhabited by various deities. Practitioners can help the circulation of their energies (Ch'i/Qi) and essences (ching/jing) through the whole body by means of inner visualization, thereby nourishing the body and prolonging their lives, hopefully forever. The "Scripture of the Yellow Court" is one of the foundational works of Chinese medical theory.[13]

BEING ONE WITH CHINESE CULTURE AND LOCAL CUSTOMS

Since Taoism evolved together with Chinese culture, some of its cultural expressions are almost indistinguishable from traditional Chinese ones. For example, except for the sculptures of Taoist deities and people dressed in Taoist garb walking around, the exterior and interior components of Taoist buildings are very similar to those of imperial, Confucian, or Chinese Buddhist buildings. Taoist architecture is not much different from mainstream Chinese architecture. On the other hand, for Taoist practitioners, a dwelling is first and foremost the setting for seeking the Tao by observing the natural phenomena, for self-cultivation, and for the pursuit of longevity and immortality. As a result, at first Taoists preferred purely natural settings, and there were grottoes and plots all over China that served as dwellings suitable for Taoists; in all there were thirty-six cavern heavens (caves where Taoists could tap into the wondrous energies of the universe) and seventy-two blessed sites where Taoists could dwell and worship. This Taoist emphasis on being one with nature has become one of the basic principles of all Chinese architecture, not just of Taoist architecture. The Taoist consideration of the Five Elements and their corresponding colors and directions (see chapters 4 and 6) has also attracted the attention of contemporary Chinese architects.

Taoist music has been patronized by the royal families and court officials of many dynasties. The Emperor Hsüan (Xuan; r. 712–756 C.E.) of the T'ang dynasty, for example, was a devout Taoist who loved Taoist rituals so much that he composed musical accompaniments for them. Played, rearranged, and even composed in the court, Taoist music was influenced by royal music in ancient China and, in turn, has preserved the ancient style of music. At the same time, Taoist music has absorbed aspects of folk music. In order to draw in the local populace and entice them to participate in religious rituals, Taoist music had to cater to the local tastes and adapt to local customs. The fact that Taoist music has taken different shapes in different regions clearly shows that Taoist music is performed both for the purpose of worship and for the purpose of entertainment. (Its function in self-cultivation and enhancing health will be discussed in chapter 10.)

Taoist music has been influenced by Buddhist music and vice versa. Taoist music and Chinese Buddhist music are similar in style, liturgical content, and instruments used, particularly in the music played during rituals. They are often performed side by side at funerals or on the fifteenth day of the seventh month of the lunar calendar. (See chapter 8 for a discussion of the significance of this holiday.)

8

Holidays

True words are not beautiful;
Beautiful words are not true.
A good man does not argue;
He who argues is not a good man.
The Way of Heaven is to benefit others and not to injure.
The Way of the sage is to act but not to compete.

—Tao Te Ching, Chapter 81

Taoism, Confucianism, and Buddhism, unlike Judaism, Christianity, and Islam, are not mutually exclusive religions. Since the three traditions openly interact in the personal and cultural lives of the Chinese, it is not surprising that they share a calendar and many holidays. There is not a Taoist calendar separate and distinct from the common Chinese calendar. In this chapter we will examine three holidays (the Chinese New Year, the Lantern Festival, and the Ghost Month) that are Taoist holidays but not exclusively Taoist. All three of these holidays are extremely important for all Chinese people.

The final section of this chapter deals with visits of deities and their worshipers to related temples. Some Taoist temples have an annual day or time period during which the major deity sculpture of the temple goes back to its "home temple" or the main deity welcomes back its offspring deity-sculptures. These visits between temples play an important role in maintaining the relationships between ancestral and descendant temples.

CHINESE NEW YEAR

The New Year starts on the first day of the first month of the lunar calendar and ends on the fifteenth day of the first month. Since there are preparatory practices that occur prior to the first day of the first lunar month, the Chinese New Year season actually encompasses a much longer period of time.

The preparation for the Chinese New Year usually starts on the twenty-third day of the twelfth month of the lunar calendar. It is believed that there is a kitchen deity dwelling in each household who guards the family, observes people's behavior, and reports to the Jade Emperor at the end of each lunar year. The Jade Emperor, in turn, punishes or rewards the family depending on their behavior. People customarily prepare a feast for the kitchen deity and his wife before he is due at the Heavenly Court of the Jade Emperor on the twenty-third day of the twelfth month. Sweets are crucial to this farewell feast because people hope that, after eating some desserts, the kitchen deity might say sweet things in his report. In some regions, malt sugar candies are used in the hope that the sticky candies will glue the kitchen deity's upper and lower teeth together and thus prevent him from saying anything bad. People in some regions prepare alcohol as well, hoping that the kitchen deity might become too drunk to remember the wrongdoings of the family. The kitchen deity supposedly returns on Chinese New Year's Eve, and naturally another feast is prepared in order to welcome him and his wife back, upon which the family also requests that he guard them well in the coming year.

Another deity who figures prominently during the Chinese New Year is the deity of wealth. Many Chinese historical figures are identified with the deity of wealth, depending upon the region of the country. The Sage Emperor Kuan Yü mentioned in chapter 5 is one of them. The deity of wealth is said to descend from heaven on the fifth day of the first month on the lunar calendar,[14] a day when most shops reopen after the New Year break. (People in Chinese societies usually take time off from work beginning with New Year's Eve and extending through the fourth day of the first month.) People typically wake up very early in the morning[15] on this day, open the door of their shops or homes, burn incense to pray to the deity of wealth, and light firecrackers to celebrate his coming. Some also hang drawings of a horse in their home, thinking that the deity of wealth might come more quickly if he has a horse.

THE JADE EMPEROR'S DESCENT AND BIRTHDAY

Another deity worshipped during the New Year period is the Jade Emperor (introduced in chapter 5). Professional Taoists would say that the Jade Emperor is not the highest deity in Taoism; though he is one of the major deities, he is ranked below the three Most Honorable Heavenly Beings: the Most Honorable Heavenly Being of Origin (Yüan-shih t'ien-tsun/Yuanshi tianzun), the Most Honorable Heavenly Being of Morality (Tao-te t'ien-tsun/Daode tianzun), and the Most Honorable Heavenly Being of Luminous Treasure (Ling-pao t'ien-tsun/

Lingbao tianzun). However, for common worshippers, the Jade Emperor is the highest god, the Sovereign of all sovereigns. He is frequently called "The One Who Is in Charge" (T'ien-kung/ Tiangong), and usually the first and biggest incense-receiving tripod seen in any Taoist temple is dedicated to him. Taoists believe that he descends to the human world once a year to acquire first-hand knowledge of human behavior. Being such an important deity, his descent and his birthday are important events.

The Jade Emperor is believed to come to the human world at the beginning of each new year to investigate people's doings so that he can reward or punish them accordingly. In traditional Chinese time calculation, the Tzu time (from 11 P.M. to 1 A.M.) is the beginning of a day; thus 11 P.M. on the thirtieth night of the twelfth month of the lunar calendar is considered the beginning of another year. The Jade Emperor is welcomed at the Tzu time of Chinese New Year's Day with an offering that consists of typical Chinese New Year presentations: a few vegetarian dishes, big red candles, and large fine paper money as described in chapter 5. Worshippers then burn incense and say prayers to the Jade Emperor, welcoming his descent to the human world, honoring his rule, and praying for his continuous protection and blessing.

The ninth day of the first month of the lunar calendar is the Jade Emperor's birthday. On this day a spectacular event is held in all Taoist temples, called "The Jade Emperor Event" (Yü-huang huei/Yuhuanghui). Many different kinds of precious incense are burned, and firecrackers are lit. A feast is, of course, indispensable in this event, just as it is a requirement at the birthday party of every respected elder in Chinese society. As a deity of such high status, the Jade Emperor is accompanied by many of the officials at the Heavenly Court; as a result the feast is extraordinarily pompous, and yet, in keeping with Taoist beliefs, all dishes have to be vegetarian (see chapter 6).

THE LANTERN FESTIVAL

The Chinese New Year period culminates with the Lantern Festival on the fifteenth day of the first month of the lunar calendar, the birthday of the Emperor of the Heavenly Realm. In order to honor him, people display specially designed colorful lanterns and pray for blessings. The Lantern Festival is one of the most festive days in the Chinese/Taoist calendar.

Lanterns, like candles, symbolize a bright future and are used to honor deities (see chapter 5). Since the Lantern Festival is held on the last day of the Chinese New Year period, it is understandable that people want to be assured of their own bright future

THE TWELVE DOUBLE-HOUR SYSTEM

Among traditional Chinese, a day consists of twelve "double-hours" instead of the twenty-four hours with which we are familiar. A day starts with the Tzu (Zi) time, which extends from 11 P.M. to 1 A.M. Wu time extends from 11 A.M. to 1 P.M. Before the Wu time is the morning, called shang-wu (shangwu, "above the Wu time"), and after the Wu time is the afternoon, called hsia-wu (xiawu, "below the Wu time"). The names of the twelve double-hours are the names of the twelve "earthly branches" mentioned in the sidebar in chapter 6. All the names of the double-hours and their corresponding Western hours are listed below:

Tzu	**(*Zi*)**	**11 P.M.–1 A.M.**
Ch'ou	**(*Chou*)**	**1 A.M.–3 A.M.**
Yin		**3 A.M.–5 A.M.**
Mao		**5 A.M.–7 A.M.**
Ch'en	**(*Chen*)**	**7 A.M.–9 A.M.**
Ssu	**(*Si*)**	**9 A.M.–11 A.M.**
Wu		**11 A.M.–1 P.M.**
Wei		**1 P.M.–3 P.M.**
Shen		**3 P.M.–5 P.M.**
Yu	**(*You*)**	**5 P.M.–7 P.M.**
Hsü	**(*Xu*)**	**7 P.M.–9 P.M.**
Hai		**9 P.M.–11 P.M.**

in the coming year. The display of all kinds of colorful lanterns symbolizes prayer for a bright future in all aspects of life, including health, wealth, friendship, marriage, parent-child relationships, and scholarly advancement. It is customary for each local government to hold a large exhibition of designer lanterns on this day. This enables people to enjoy very expensive lanterns that an average individual or family could not afford. Along with the lantern exhibition, there may also be parades, singing, dancing, and acrobatic performances. These performances are dedicated to the Emperor of the Heavenly Realm, and they are also for the people's pleasure. People also enjoy "lantern-riddles"—riddles stuck on the surface of lanterns for people to guess while enjoying the different lantern designs. Those who are *bright* enough to solve these riddles return home with some rewards and the assurance of their "bright" future in the coming year.

Another integral part of the Lantern Festival is a ball-shaped sticky-rice dumpling called yüan-hsiao (yuanxiao). Yüan-hsiao is one of the dishes included in the offering to the Emperor of the Heavenly Realm because of its symbolic meanings. The round shape stands for all-inclusiveness and perfection, and the stickiness and elasticity of the sticky-rice represent well-adjusted interpersonal relationships. The most popular fillings of yüan-hsiao are black sesame paste, red bean paste, peanut paste, and ground pork, although the yüan-hsiao with ground pork filling usually is not used by strict Taoists due to their vegetarian diet.

THE GHOST MONTH

The Emperors of the Three Realms mentioned in chapter 5 govern and protect the heavenly realm, the earthly realm, and the watery realm. People pray to the Emperor of the Heavenly Realm for the delivery of blessings, to the Emperor of the Earthly Realm for the pardoning of wrongdoings, and to the Emperor of the Watery Realm for the dissolution of dangers. The Lantern Festival is the birthday of the Emperor of the Heavenly Realm, while the Ghost Month centers around the birthday of the Emperor of the Earthly Realm, which is on the fifteenth day of the seventh month of the lunar calendar. Theoretically, the Emperor of the Watery Realm is as important as the other two Emperors, but his birthday, the fifteenth day of the tenth month, is not an important holiday.

The seventh month of the lunar calendar is called Ghost Month (kuei-yüeh/guiyue). It is believed that the gates of hell are opened on the first day of this month, and all ghosts are allowed to return to the human world to visit their loved ones until the end of the month, when the gates of hell are once again closed. During this month, people make offerings of food and paper money (paper money is believed to circulate in the underworld) for their ancestors or recently deceased relatives to enjoy. Taoists believe that some ghosts do not have any living loved ones to care for them, hence they prepare abundant amounts of food and paper money offerings so that all ghosts can be cared for. Some people make offerings for all ghosts because they are worried that their own kind-hearted, well-behaved ancestors will be bullied by malicious ghosts and be deprived of food; others fear that the uncared-for ghosts, lacking better things to do, might come to harass them. Whether out of love, worry, or fear, the practice of preparing food for ghosts demonstrates Taoist belief in the existence of spirits and the expenditure of Taoist effort in building good relationships with the spirit world.

Taoists celebrate the birthday of the Emperor of the Earthly Realm on the fifteenth day of Ghost Month. Among Buddhists, this same day is known as Ulambana (in Chinese it is transliterated as Yü-lan-p'en/Yulanpen; in Japanese, O-bon). Since in both religions this day is associated with the alleviation of the suffering of those in hell and since many Chinese are simultaneously Buddhist and Taoist, it is not uncommon that professional Taoists and Buddhist monks and nuns stand side by side on this day performing rituals and reciting scriptures and liturgies. This is a day when all those in the underworld are cared for and prayed for, and most Chinese people, even those who do not consider themselves religious, prepare an extraordinarily lavish feast and then burn stick incense and invite all ghosts who pass by to enjoy the food. People who lean more toward Taoism than Buddhism make a separate offering to the Emperor of the Earthly Realm and recite scriptures and liturgies on behalf of their deceased loved ones, praying for their pardon. As further evidence of the mixing of Taoism and Buddhism, it is interesting to note that Buddhist bodhisattvas (for example, Avalokiteśvara, the bodhisattva who comes to the rescue of all sufferers, and Kşitigarbha, the bodhisattva who swore to save all those in hell) are mentioned in the texts recited to celebrate the birthday of the Taoist Emperor of the Earthly Realm.

DEITIES VISITING HOME TEMPLES

In Taoism, deities migrate when people migrate. From time to time there are large-scale migrations due to tyranny, wars, natural disasters, or the pursuit of a better life. When people are about to move to a new place, it is customary for them to go to the temple they usually visit, pray to the major deity (in Taoist temples, there is usually more than one deity), and ask the deity to protect them wherever they go. When a group of people eventually settles in a new place, they create another sculpture of the deity and build a temple for it. In Taoism, places of origin are highly valued, and hence, even after generations pass and the worshippers in an offshoot temple do not have any personal memory of the migration of their ancestors, the original temple is still highly valued and recognized as the "home temple." People still pay homage to the original sculpture of the deity at least once a year, either on the deity's birthday, on the day the deity is said to have acquired immortality, or on any other day of particular significance. The home temple is also host to a huge event to welcome back the deity sculptures from all offshoot temples.

When there are no obstacles to deter the sculpture of the deity in the offshoot temple from visiting home, it is carried back to the home temple while traditional Chinese festive music is performed and firecrackers are lit all along the route. When there are obstacles prohibiting such a procession, the sculpture is turned to face the direction of the home temple, and worshippers

FROM THE TAOIST TRADITION

Statue of Lao-tzu, the legendary founder of Taoism, riding a water buffalo. Lao-tzu, who lived during the Spring and Autumn period (770–476 B.C.E.), is the supposed author of the Tao Te Ching, the single most revered scripture in both philosophical and religious Taoism.

Lung-Shan Temple, Taipei, Taiwan. Taoist practitioners offer snacks or fruits and paper money, and burn either incense or candles to honor any number of the 166 deities who are worshipped at the temple.

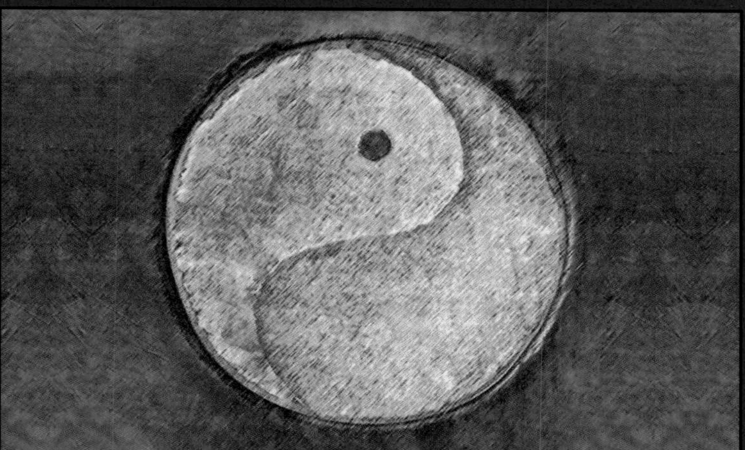

The relationship between opposites, or yin and yang, provides Chinese people with a framework by which to understand and analyze all phenomena in the world. Yin is represented by the darker section of the circle, while yang is depicted by the lighter section. In this world, there is neither pure brightness nor pure darkness, neither pure good nor pure evil.

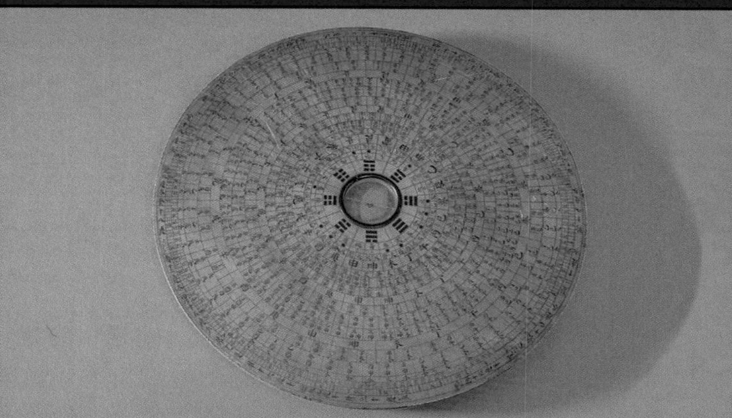

Feng shui, the Chinese art of living in harmony with the environment, was developed thousands of years ago in southern China. Feng shui compasses like this one were used to determine the best location to build a house; one where yin and yang and the Five Elements were harmoniously balanced, which would diminish one's chances of becoming ill.

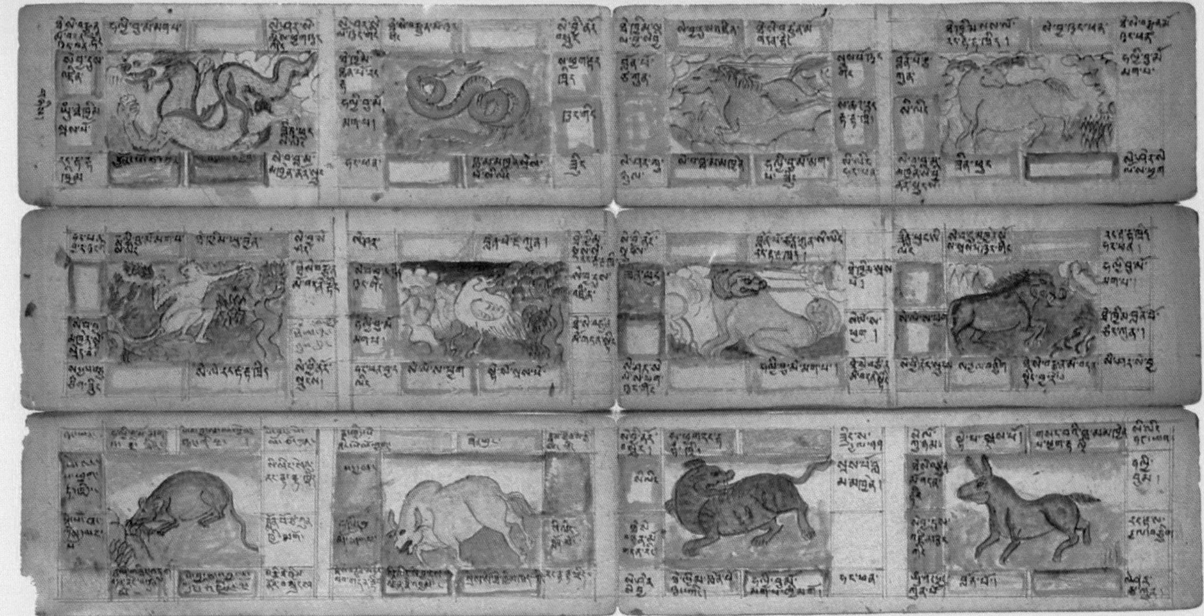

The twelve animals of the Chinese Zodiac are represented here on a late-eighteenth-century Tibetan manuscript. Each animal sign recurs every twelve years and the animals are associated with different personality traits. For instance, it is advantageous to be born during the year of the dragon, because it symbolizes freedom, power, fortune, and high social status.

Li Po (Li Bo), the "Immortal of Poetry," lived during the T'ang dynasty (618–907 C.E.) and expressed his great love for nature and the environment through his poems. Li Po was also designated of the "Highest Purity," which is the honorary title of one of the three highest deities in Taoism.

Homage to the First Principle, East Wall Painting, Royal Ontario Museum, Toronto. Created in the early fourteenth century, this painting portrays a procession of Chinese deities, including the Yellow Emperor, who is traditionally regarded as one of the earliest rulers in Chinese history and the single most important foundational figure of Chinese civilization.

Gu Kaizhi (c. 345–406 c.e.), who lived during the Eastern Chin dynasty, is among the outstanding Taoist painters. This painting, housed at the British Museum in London, depicts one of nine scenes collectively known as the *Admonitions to the Court Ladies*. The scenes detail the excessive behavior of a Chinese empress.

Housed at the Musée des Arts Asiatiques-Guimet, Paris, *Through the Autumn Mountains with a Lute in Hand*, conveys the Taoist ideal of being one with nature and finding the Tao, or "the way."

all pray facing the same direction. Consider, for example, the home temple of a female deity named "The Heavenly Empress" (T'ien-hou/Tianhou), which stands in mainland China but has descendant temples on the island of Taiwan. The Heavenly Empress is depicted as a mother-like protector who looks after fishermen and seamen in particular; her nickname is "The Mother-Ancestress" (Ma-tsu/Mazu). The Heavenly Empress was originally worshipped along the southeast coast of China, but because many Chinese people have migrated to Taiwan over the past several hundred years, she is also worshipped throughout Taiwan. During the period when relations between Communist China and Nationalist Taiwan were strained, worshippers of the Heavenly Empress in Taiwan could not physically visit the home temple in Southeast China, so they paid homage to the original sculpture by facing toward the sculpture. Since Taiwanese are now allowed to visit China via Hong Kong, trips are arranged so that the offshoot deity sculptures and their worshippers can visit the home temple. These homecoming trips are usually arranged once every several years due to financial considerations. Firecrackers are set off (and music is performed) only along a small section of the route because it is impossible to have them in the airport or on airplanes.

9

Memories

There was something undifferentiated and yet complete,
Which existed before Heaven and Earth.
Soundless and formless,
it depends on nothing and does not change.
It operates everywhere and is free from danger.
It may be considered the mother of the universe.
I do not know its name; I call it Tao.

—Tao Te Ching, Chapter 25

The reader will recall that the period of the Eastern Chou dynasty was a particularly troublesome time that engendered various philosophies (see chapter 2). Besides the creation of the Tao Te Ching and the Chuang-tzu, there were many other schools of religious and philosophical thought. Toward the end of the Warring States period, there was a tendency for each school to incorporate the thoughts of different schools; this tendency was continued by scholars in the Han dynasty, even though by then Confucianism had been declared the state ideology. The Taoist political philosophy upheld by the ruling elite was not the same as the religious Taoism of the common people, but different elements from each were gradually integrated into one system. By the start of the T'ang (Tang) dynasty (618–907 C.E.), Taoism had successfully integrated so many strains of thought that it appealed to the sentiments of both aristocrats and commoners. Moreover, the imperial family of the T'ang dynasty, with the same surname as Lao-tzu, claimed Lao-tzu as their ancestor and retrospectively honored him as the "the Sage Ancestor-Emperor of the Abstruse Origin." Thousands of state-sponsored Taoist temples were built throughout the T'ang dynasty, and more and more local deities were incorporated into Taoism. Taoism became a major religion that rivaled Buddhism, while Confucianism remained the official state ideology. Interacting with one another for several hundred years, the Three Teachings—Taoism, Confucianism, and Buddhism—were further integrated on the theoretical level by the Neo-Confucians in the Sung (Song) dynasty (960–1279) and the Ming dynasty (1368–1644). At this point, it was no longer possible to completely disentangle the Three Teachings, and they all became essential features of Chinese culture.

THE CONTESTING AND BLENDING OF SCHOOLS IN THE PRE-CH'IN ERA

Taoism actually refers to the mixture of several different theories, doctrines, and practices. Most relevant to our discussion is

Lao-tzu's philosophy. Many Western scholars think it is based in mysticism, and this is partly true, because the language of the Tao Te Ching is very obscure; however, most Chinese people read Lao-tzu as political philosophy. In the Tao Te Ching, when the term "the Sage" appears, it almost always means "the ideal ruler" or at least "the preferred ruler." The book Chuang-tzu, on the other hand, is obviously not about the art of ruling. As mentioned in chapter 2, Chuang-tzu was more concerned with the art of protecting life from a commoner's point of view. Thus, originally Lao-tzu and Chuang-tzu had different perspectives, even though in later times people associated the two and their philosophies.

With regard to how the chaos of the time could be stopped, Lao-tzu and Chuang-tzu were indeed very close, and they were both at odds with Confucianism and Legalism. In simplest terms, Confucianism proposed that the order and values of an earlier time had to be restored in order to end the turmoil and distress of the present time. In contrast, Legalism espoused that the enhancement of the ruler's power and authority was the most effective way to end the turmoil and destruction. Thus both Confucianism and Legalism coped with the chaotic world by reinforcing or establishing more behavioral codes. However, both the Tao Te Ching and the Chuang-tzu disagreed with this viewpoint and taught instead that what went wrong with the world was precisely the rulers' obsession with establishing rules and norms. They taught that it was against nature for anyone to arbitrarily create behavioral codes and then try to coerce others to behave accordingly. Toward the end of the Warring States period, however, some works incorporated Confucianism and Legalism together with philosophical Taoism. For instance, although Kuan Chung (Guan Zhong) was commonly considered a Legalist, some chapters of Kuan-tzu (Guanzi), a work attributed to him, conveyed the Taoist concern for following nature. Hsün-tzu's (Xunzi) work, the third most famous Confucian text in the Pre-Ch'in era, likewise expressed the same Taoist concern.

In addition to philosophical Taoism, Confucianism, and Legalism, Kuan-tzu and Hsün-tzu also integrated the Yin-Yang and Five-Element theories. The Yin-Yang and Five-Element theories are generally recognized as part of Taoism today, though they have probably existed since the beginning of Chinese civilization. There was a Yin-Yang school in the Warring States period, but no one has been identified as its founder. People usually cite *Tsou Yen* (Zou Yan; c. 305–240 B.C.E.) as a representative thinker of the school but no work of his is extant. The founder of the Five-Element theory is also unknown. We should note that both the Yin-Yang and Five-Element theories can be found in almost all of the ancient philosophical schools, because both are indigenous to ancient China.[16]

THE EMERGENCE OF RELIGIOUS TAOISM

During the Han dynasty, various philosophical schools were further integrated with philosophical Taoism by scholars, while religious Taoism took shape among commoners. The Han dynasty followed several hundred years of wars in the Eastern Chou and the tyrannical rule of the Ch'in (Qin) dynasty (221–206 B.C.E.). In the first few decades, the rulers of the Han claimed that they were ruling by "the method of Huang and Lao." The ideal was to take care of the people, as Huang-ti did, and stop meddling with people's lives by imposing wars and regulations, as the Tao Te Ching had suggested. At the same time, scholars continued to blend the thoughts of various schools, and the declaration elevating Confucianism to the state ideology encouraged this trend. Many of the Confucian scholars serving as court officials believed in the Yin-Yang and Five-Element theories, emphasized the importance of being one with nature, and provided emperors with knowledge that could be used in the development of ruling strategies.

Outside the imperial court, some commoners also believed in Huang-ti and Lao-tzu, though their concern was the pursuit of a long life and not strategies for ruling. Serving as the specialists among the Huang-Lao Tao believers were a group of people known as fang-shih (fangshi) and later called Tao-shih (Daoshi), that is, professional Taoists. The Tao-shih were not philosophers nor were they erudite in different schools of thoughts; rather they basically functioned as mediums, sorcerers, and magicians. In other words, the Tao-shih were people who had the ability to communicate with or even manipulate the invisible powers in the universe on behalf of their fellow human beings. For these professional Taoists, the term "Tao" referred to the order of the supernatural world or the will of supernatural beings, including people's ancestors. As a religion, Taoism was more akin to Chinese folk beliefs[17] than to the school of philosophy inspired by Lao-tzu and Chuang-tzu. However, the "Tao" in the philosophical sense, that is, the infinite and incomprehensible origin of the universe as described in the Tao Te Ching and the Chuang-tzu, gradually entered popular beliefs as well.

In the first century, Chang Tao-ling declared himself the "Heavenly Master" and founded a religious organization, popularly called the "Heavenly Master's Tao," or the "Five Pecks of Rice Tao." The "Five Pecks of Rice Tao" was similar to the "Huang-Lao Tao," though Chang Tao-ling added a moral dimension to it. Besides drawing talismans and dispelling diseases as did other Tao-shih, the Heavenly Master and his associates also taught their followers to repent for their own mistakes, cultivate their character, and to do more charity work. The seemingly bizarre requirement of handing in five pecks of rice to become a member of the organization may have simply been a way to collect and redistribute food to the needy. Chang Tao-ling also incorporated folk beliefs and practices from different regions, which helped the "Five Pecks of Rice Tao" spread throughout China a century later.

Approximately one century after the establishment of the "Heavenly Master's Tao," another religious Taoist organization, called the "T'ai-p'ing Tao" (Taiping Dao), emerged. This organization gained its name because of the scripture it affirmed, the T'ai-p'ing Ching (Taipingjing) or the Scripture of the Ultimate Equilibrium. Though the T'ai-p'ing Tao organization existed for only a short time, in less than twenty years it recruited several hundred thousand followers and instigated a large-scale uprising against the Han dynasty. The spreading of both the "Five Pecks of Rice Tao" and the "T'ai-p'ing Tao" demonstrated that religious Taoism was closely in touch with commoners' day-to-day thoughts and concerns. The commoners then adopted the term "Tao" and integrated the Yin-Yang and Five-Element theories, just as the ruling class had done previously. Thus, what was originally a strategy for ruling became something that could improve the lives of the oppressed. It endowed them with strength and legitimized their rebellion.

THE EXPANSION OF TAOISM IN THE T'ANG DYNASTY

Other Pre-Ch'in schools appeared to die out when Confucianism became the state ideology during the Han dynasty, but in reality elements from other schools infiltrated into Confucianism and continued on. Moreover, on the popular level, the ancient folk beliefs, such as ancestor worship and the Yin-Yang and Five-Element theories, converged with the pursuit of longevity, the quest for a better society, and some of the philosophical ideas of Lao-tzu to form a belief system that appealed to the common people. By the time of the establishment of the T'ang dynasty, Taoism had spread so widely that many rulers of different dynasties found it beneficial to tap into that religion for the purpose of consolidating their regimes. One peculiar example was the T'ang ruling family's claim to be the descendents of Lao-tzu.

The rulers of the T'ang dynasty had the surname Li, which is the same as Lao-tzu's surname. But Lao-tzu was not simply deemed a remote relative who carried the same family name; in the standard history compiled by the T'ang state, a new family tree was constructed that named Lao-tzu as the founding ancestor of the T'ang ruling house. Out of reverence for their renowned sage-ancestor, the T'ang imperial family not only gave Lao-tzu honorable titles such as "the Sage Ancestor-Emperor of the Abstruse Origin" but also decreed the establishment of thousands of temples to worship him. The T'ang family built thousands of Taoist monasteries and nunneries throughout its territory and favored Taoist priests with high positions in the government. The Tao Te Ching was elevated into the curriculum of the Imperial Examination for Prospective Officials and ranked first among all of the Confucian Classical texts. A new examination system was created whereby scholars in Taoism could be qualified for civil service. Twelve out of the 207 princesses in the T'ang dynasty renounced their aristocratic life to be Taoist nuns. In fact, the bond between Taoism and the T'ang imperial family was so strong that the T'ang royal house seemed to be the most religiously oriented imperial clan and the most devoted disciples of Lao-tzu in all of Chinese history.

The T'ang rulers' sponsorship of religious Taoism served more than one purpose. First, religious Taoist organizations met people's needs (such as the need for medical treatment and the need for showing respect to their ancestors), yet could also justify people's right to express their dissent (such as the T'ai-p'ing Tao uprising). By incorporating Taoism and supporting it with the state's resources, the T'ang rulers turned a force that could be used against them into a force that could be used to support their regime. Second, the Taoist deities had been organized based on the model of the Han bureaucratic system, with minor deities taking orders from major deities, and all of the deities being subordinated to one supreme deity. The whole conceptualization of the relations between deities had the effect of legitimizing the bureaucratic system. More specifically, the T'ang rulers' act of sponsoring religious Taoism added legitimacy to their regime. Just as Lao-tzu was the "Emperor of the Abstruse Origin" and ruled over other celestial beings by following the Tao, his descendants, the T'ang ruling family, were ruling the people justly by helping spread the Tao. Third, Buddhism was attracting more and more believers, and had inadvertently threatened the state's status as the one and only authority. Sponsorship of Taoism counterbalanced the growing Buddhist influence by treating Taoism as the indigenous Chinese religion and Buddhism as the foreign religion. The T'ang state even held public debates between Taoists and Buddhists on several occasions. At the same time, the emperors and the state officials continued to adhere to the Confucian-Legalist ideology, because their primary concern was maintaining authoritative status and ruling effectively. Throughout T'ang history, there were Confucian scholars who consistently denounced both Taoism and Buddhism and wanted to reserve the term "Sage" for Confucius alone.

A BLENDING TOGETHER OF THE THREE TEACHINGS IN THE SUNG AND MING DYNASTIES

The power relation among the Three Teachings in the T'ang dynasty was intriguing. On the one hand, Confucians, Taoists,

THE DEMOLITION OF BUDDHISM IN THE NAME OF TAOISM

When Buddhism entered China around the beginning of the Common Era, various dynastic rulers were concerned about the rapid rise of Buddhist authority. Consequently, the rulers claimed Taoism as their indigenous religion and rejected Buddhism as an alien intrusion. Under the pretense of protecting the native religion, three emperors in Chinese history decreed that Buddhist temples, monasteries, nunneries, and the arts should be demolished. These three emperors, coincidently, were all posthumously given the character "Wu" in their title, thus declaring their obsession with the use of military power. The three emperors were the Great Emperor Wu of the Northern Wei dynasty (r. 423–452 C.E.), the Emperor Wu of the Northern Chou dynasty (r. 560–578), and the Emperor Wu of the T'ang dynasty (r. 840–846). Chinese historians call these three waves of demolition of Buddhism the "Disaster of the Three Wu's."

and Buddhists borrowed terms from each other and demonstrated the possibility of cooperation. On the other hand, they were at odds with each other partly because it was difficult for the ruling class to agree with the common people's ideology. Indeed, it was even more difficult for the advocates of an indigenous religion to overcome the racial barrier and to embrace a foreign philosophy (Buddhism). During the Sung dynasty, however, things changed. Taoism as a folk religion and Taoism as a ruling philosophy had united under the sponsorship of the T'ang state. Since Confucianism and Taoism both considered the Book of Change (I-Ching/Yijing) to be one of their classics, it became impossible for the two religions to remain strangers with one another. In the meantime, Buddhism had been part of Chinese culture for long enough that its foreign nature had gradually worn off. The mutual borrowing of terms between Buddhism and Taoism further paved the way for the blending of the two religions.

The group of people who contributed most to the blending together of the Three Teachings were the Neo-Confucians. The Confucian scholar Chu Hsi was one of them. Actually, the term "Neo-Confucianism" is quite misleading. First, Neo-Confucianism could also be called "Neo-Taoism" or "Neo-Buddhism," because the thoughts developed at the time were in fact a mixture of Confucianism, Taoism, and Buddhism. Second, Neo-Confucianism is very different from Confucianism. Sung scholars called Neo-Confucianism "the Study of the Universal Logic" (Li Hsüeh/Li Xue), while Ming scholars named it "the Study of the Mind" (Hsin Hsüeh/Xin Xue). Sung and Ming scholars investigated the logic by which the universe operates, usually using Buddhist and Taoist terms, and then argued that the embodiment of the universal logic would be the values and behavioral codes Confucius taught. This blending of the Three Teachings probably occurred among the mostly illiterate commoners long before the rise of what is called Neo-Confucianism. Folk literature since the Han dynasty often illustrated the tendency to combine the three religions, but when the blending was done by the scholar-officials who were well educated, it indicated that the Three Teachings had intertwined with one another on a deeper level. Beyond this point in time even people who were trained to be Confucians would also affirm the teachings of Taoism and Buddhism.

10

Taoism in the World Today

Tao is eternal and has no name.
Though its simplicity seems insignificant,
none in the world can master it.
If political leaders would hold on to it,
all things would submit to them spontaneously.

—Tao Te Ching, Chapter 32

Taoism has provided Chinese people with a framework for understanding the world and has been a cornerstone of Chinese medicine, martial arts, alchemy, astrology, philosophy, literature, and the arts. In modern times, many of the functions of Taoism have been replaced by scientific studies, and many Taoist beliefs and practices are dismissed as superstitions. If in the past Chinese people did not exclusively identify themselves as Taoists, today many are eager to disassociate themselves with their Taoist roots lest they be branded backward and superstitious. The influence of Taoism on the lives of Chinese people, however, is still clearly evident. In addition, an ever-increasing number of people turn to Taoism for consolation and inspiration when faced with the dead-end presented by materialism and overdevelopment. The understanding of Tao as the nurturing mother of everything in the cosmos compels people to adopt a nonanthropocentric worldview compatible with contemporary ecological perspectives. Tao's continuous self-balancing movement suggests that people practice moderation and exercise regularly. Taoist theories also form the basis of music therapy, which is a rapidly growing field. More significantly, the depiction of Tao as a mother who lets her children be themselves teaches the followers of Tao to respect differences. The Taoist notions of relative truth combined with the all-encompassing nature of the Tao encourage Taoists to be inclusive, embracing other religions and philosophies.

CARE FOR OTHER FORMS OF LIFE

Tao is the generator, nurturer, and caretaker of the world and the myriad of things in it. In the Taoist worldview, human beings do not have dominion over the nonhuman world; instead, they are placed side by side with nonhuman beings. Humans are simply one of the myriad of things that are generated, nurtured, and cared for by Tao. Since "virtue" in Taoism is defined as being one with Tao, humans are encouraged to emulate the "behavior" of Tao and take good care of other forms of existence as well as their fellow human beings. In a text attributed to Lao-Tzu entitled the One Hundred and Eighty Precepts, Taoists are admonished to abstain from all kinds of killing and hurting, particularly in the spring and the summer, when animals and plants are growing. According to the same text, Taoists should not disturb animals during their hibernation, climb up trees to reach into nests lest the eggs are broken, or set snares to catch animals. The Taoist ethos is to nurture things and let them be themselves.

Taoists extend this care to forms that are invisible. All of the special days in the Chinese/Taoist calendar are days for humans to contact and take care of spirits, including deities and ancestors. The Ghost Month, which culminates on the fifteenth day of the seventh month of the lunar calendar, is a time for Taoists to take care of all ghosts, since ghosts are merely another form of existence and are part of the natural world that human beings inhabit. The "birthdays" of different deities also create opportunities for humans to build relationships with nonhumans. Even though Taoists consider deities to be a superior form of being far more powerful than humans, humans can still express their care and build a rapport with the deities by preparing feasts for them. As a matter of fact, Taoist practitioners try to communicate with and express their care and gratitude for the spiritual world at least twice a month: On the first and the fifteenth days of every month, Taoists regularly make offerings to deities, ancestors, and other spirits.

The Taoist worldview values animate beings as well as the inanimate natural environment upon which they depend. Being one of the myriad of sentient beings in the world, Taoists are expected to respect nature; the environment that makes every form of life possible. The One Hundred and Eighty Precepts attributed to Lao-tzu admonishes people not to willfully chop down trees, pluck flowers, or change natural landscapes; it also exhorts individuals to make adjustments in order to fit into nature rather than to exploit nature to accommodate their need or greed. Feng shui is a theory and practice that seeks to tap into the circulating cosmic energies to improve human life. Its practitioners often voice their serious reservations about the damages done to the natural world in the name of economic development. The belief in the correspondence between the natural world and the human world implies that the well-being of people is also negatively affected if the natural world suffers undue change.

The Taoist worldview implicitly rejects worldviews that depict humanity in opposition to nature or that pit spirit against matter. Human beings, nonhuman beings, and the nonanimate natural world are all generated by Tao and are obligated to take care of one another. The nonanthropocentric worldview of Taoism has resounding ecological implications and therefore has drawn much attention from those concerned about the environment.

BALANCE OF THE FIVE ELEMENTS AND THE YIN AND YANG

In Taoism, the human body is often called the "microcosm." The human body is a miniature mirror image of the larger "macrocosm" of the universe. The body operates according to the very same principles on which the whole universe operates. Just as there are Yin, Yang, and the Five Elements in the macrocosm, each is present in the human body as well. For example, according to Chinese medical theory (which is based on Taoism), five of the internal organs of the human body correspond to the Five Elements and are Yang in nature: the liver is of the nature of Yang Wood; the kidneys, of Yang Water; the lungs, of Yang Metal; the heart, of Yang Fire; and the spleen, of Yang Earth. Other internal organs correspond to the Five Elements and are Yin in nature: the gallbladder is of the nature of Yin Wood; the bladder, of Yin Water; the lower intestines, of Yin Metal; the small intestines, of Yin Fire; and the stomach, of Yin Earth. These internal organs have mutually enhancing and mutually weakening relations, just as the Five Elements do. For example, an overactive liver is often accompanied by a stomachache, since Wood (liver) works against Earth (stomach). Thus, instead of using a painkiller, Chinese medicine practitioners may choose to treat a stomachache with a medicine that can regulate the function of the liver.

Taoism provides dietary suggestions and recommends moderation and exercise. Taoist dietary suggestions are also very closely related to the Five-Element theory because both seasons and tastes are associated with the Five Elements. In the winter, for instance, Chinese medicine recommends that people reduce their intake of salty food and eat more bitter food. Winter is associated with Water, which is also associated with the salty taste, and Water works against Fire, which is associated with the heart and the bitter taste. Taking too much salty food (Water) is thus believed to harm the heart, while eating more bitter food (Fire) is believed to prevent heart attack. More importantly, Tao's attempt to keep balance in all things inspires Taoists to practice self-moderation and keeps them away from extremes. Having too much of something cannot produce long-term well-being. On the contrary, once the balance is broken, undesirable results tend to occur. For instance, some people may experience happiness when eating sweets, but having too much sweet food (Earth) may enervate the kidneys and the bladder (Water) and thus result in an undesirable physical condition, which leads to unhappiness. The key to a healthy and long life is balance, both between the Yin and the Yang and among the Five Elements; therefore people need to practice moderation and avoid extremes in order to enjoy a lasting quality of life. In addition, as noted in chapter 4, Tao is continuously moving, and this continuous movement is the reason it can keep generating the myriad of things in the world. Thus, human beings, in trying to model themselves after Tao, should likewise keep moving, exercise regularly, and lead an active and productive life at all times.

Taoism influences trends in modern music therapy. While in Western music there are seven basic tones, in Taoist or traditional Chinese music there are five. (A person who cannot sing is described in Chinese as "not having the complete set of the five tones.") In Taoism, it has long been held that music can improve physical and mental health. Each of the five tones can energize its corresponding set of internal organs. The kung (gong) tone (the equivalent of the C note in Western music), for example, helps the spleen and the stomach to function well, and the shang tone (the equivalent of the D note in Western music) enhances the conditions of the lungs and the lower intestines. Since people's dispositions are also associated with the Five Elements, it is believed that the five tones can be therapeutic to different personality types. A person of the Earth-type personality, for instance, can benefit from music of the chih (zhi) tone (the equivalent of the G note in Western music), for chih is Fire, and Fire helps Earth. Music therapy has become an academic subject in the West, and many Taoist music-therapy kits have been developed and are now available on the market.

RELIGIOUS INCLUSIVISM

It is commonly assumed that the polytheism of Taoism is simply an extension of the "animistic" belief ascribed to ancient folk religions.[18] In other words, the belief in many deities is often considered primitive or even backward. While this assumption has been discredited by religious studies scholars, it remains a part of popular polemics. According to many monotheists, those who believe in only one deity, the belief in many deities indicates a lack of capacity for systematic reasoning on the part of common people. Upon closer investigation, however, it is very clear that the central doctrines of Taoism demand the acceptance of difference and the inclusion of other philosophies. Thus, Taoist systematic reasoning supports religious inclusivism, that is, the acceptance of a variety of beliefs. In an age when religious differences have again emerged as a major source of conflict, perhaps the world has something to learn from the Tao depicted by Lao-tzu and Chuang-tzu.

As stated in chapter 2, Lao-tzu and Chuang-tzu lived in a time when rulers tried to impose their will on others. Some rulers resorted to military power and inflicted suffering on thousands in order to establish their own way as the way, while other rulers implemented hundreds of regulations in order to keep their subjects under control. Though the latter may not have waged wars, they were not much different from the former in that both kinds of rulers claimed authority, demanded obedience, and attempted to change the world to fit their own image. Each sought to establish a hierarchical system and a power structure centering on him, and each thought he alone represented the one true way. In response to this type of reasoning, Lao-tzu proposed a different strategy. Countering the image of an authoritative patriarch with unchallengeable absolute power over the people, Lao-tzu portrayed the ultimate reality as a nurturing mother whose only wish was to see her children flourish on their own. Tao nurtures a myriad of different things but is not concerned with her own possessive or authoritative status; she cares for all beings but does not interfere with their lives. The Sage emulates Tao and does not force others to conform to one set of norms. The Sage accepts the fact that there are many differences between people.

To accept these differences does not mean that the gap cannot be bridged between differing views, nor does it mean that different forms of existence should not try to communicate with one another. In the Chuang-tzu (Nan-hua Ching), it is affirmed that millions of different things are all manifestations of one and the same Tao. In this sense, all are equally true and equally valuable; however, nothing contains Tao, though Tao contains everything. In other words, no single thing fully manifests the whole reality; each and every one of the myriad of things reflects reality only partially. As such, all differences are equally valid, and all truths proposed by different schools are true, and yet they are true only from a particular conventional perspective that is limited. Another way of expressing this idea is to say that no one has a monopoly on truth, for no single perspective contains the whole Tao and none is absolutely right. The legacy of Chuang-tzu is that people should always keep relativity in mind and avoid creating a hierarchical system in which the value perceived by the self is the only true value. Chuang-tzu's thoughts also teach people to remember that on the ultimate level all are one and to replace competition with mutual caring.

Both Lao-tzu's and Chuang-tzu's understandings of Tao promote religious inclusivism. Their teachings encourage people to accept differences as differences without creating any opposition between one's self and others who are different. As a result, Taoism has incorporated many of the deities from different traditions but those deities are not necessarily subordinated to one another. Granted, since Taoist deities were organized based on the model of the bureaucratic system of the state, some deities were elevated to be higher than others. But the hierarchy is a loose one, and most of the deities are not ranked against each other. This may seem strange to those accustomed to political or religious hierarchies because the establishment of a hierarchy requires the elevation of a particular viewpoint or power above all other viewpoints or powers. However, Taoists are taught not to consider one deity as above or below another deity. They are taught to accept and include many gods without ranking them; each serves a different purpose and all are needed and work together to form a whole. To a non-Taoist, this system may seem riddled with inconsistencies and contradictions. However, to understand Taoism, one needs to understand the Taoist view of opposite things that exist in nature and that together compose a whole; both sides are equally important and necessary. Tao speaks in and through apparent inconsistencies and contradictions.

CHRONOLOGY & TIMELINE

Legendary period

c. 3000–2100 B.C.E. The Eight Trigrams were first drawn by a legendary figure named Fu-hsi (Fuxi); reign of Yellow Emperor (Huang-ti).

Hsia dynasty

c. 2100–1600 B.C.E.

Shang dynasty

c. 1600–1050 B.C.E.

Western Chou dynasty

c. 1050–771 B.C.E. I-Ching written.

Spring and Autumn period

770–476 B.C.E. Tao Te Ching written.

c. 3000–2100 B.C.E.
Eight Trigrams first drawn

c. 531 B.C.E.
Lao-tzu born

c. Sixth century B.C.E.
Tao Te Ching written

c.e. 25–220
"Five Pecks of Rice Tao" (first Taoist religious organization) established

BCE (BC) | CE (AD)

3000 1500 300 | 300

c. 1050–771 B.C.E.
I-Ching written

350 B.C.E.
Chuang-tzu further develops Taoist philosophy

First Century C.E.
(Taipingjing) or the Scripture of the Ultimate Equilibrium compiled

Warring States period

476–221 B.C.E. Chuang-tzu (Nan-hua Ching) written, traditionally by Chuang-tzu; Lieh-tzu; Tsou Yen, representative thinker of the Yin-Yang school.

Ch'in (Qin) dynasty

221–206 B.C.E.

Western Han dynasty

206 B.C.E.–8 C.E. Practice of the "Method of Huang and Lao" and the emergence of "Huang-Lao Tao" (cult).

Eastern Han dynasty

25–220 Emergence of the "Five Pecks of Rice Tao"

307–365 or 321–379
"Saint of Calligraphy" Wang Hsi-chih

386–589
Tao-shih (professional Taoists) established

1966–1976
Taoists persecuted during China's Cultural Revolution

500 1000 1500 2000

701–762
"Immortal of Poetry" Li Po

c. 712–756
Under Emperor Hsüan, Taoist Canon composed for the first time

960–1279
Three compilations of the Taoist Canon

1436
Tao-tsang reprinted

1911
China becomes a republic

	under the leadership of Chang Tao-ling; T'ai-p'ing Ching (earliest religious Taoist scripture) and the T'ai-p'ing Tao (religious organization) established; uprising under the leadership of Chang Chiao (Zhang Jiao).
Three Kingdoms period	
220–280	Kuan Yü (Guan Yu), the sage emperor.
Eastern Chin dynasty	
317–420	The burgeoning of Hsüan Hsüeh (Xuan Xue), sometimes translated as "Neo-Taoism"; Taoist theorist Ke Hung (c. 283–343); the "Saint of Calligraphy" Wang Hsi-chih (307–365 or 321–379); landscape painter Ku K'ai-chih (345–406); landscape poet Hsieh Ling-Yün (385–433).
Northern/Southern dynasties	
386–589	Tao-shih (professional Taoists) established.
T'ang (Tang) dynasty	
618–907	Lao-tzu revered as the Sage-Ancestor of the T'ang royal family; first compilation of the Taoist Canon; the "Immortal of Poetry" Li Po (701–762); court painter Wu Tao-tzu (active c. 710–760).
Sung (Song) dynasty	
960–1279	Three compilations of the Taoist Canon; the integration of the Three Teachings under the umbrella term Li Hsüeh (Li Xue), commonly translated as "Neo-Confucianism."
Chin (Jin) dynasty	
1115–1234	Fifth compilation of the Taoist Canon.

Southern Sung dynasty

1127–1279 Synthesizer of Neo-Confucianism Chu Hsi (1130–1200).

Yüan (Yuan) dynasty

1279–1368 Sixth compilation of the Taoist Canon; *Tao-shih* Chiu Ch'u-chi (Qiu Chuji; 1148–1227); *Tao-shih* Chang San-feng (Zhang Sanfeng; 1247– c. 1324).

Ming dynasty

1368–1644 Seventh compilation of the Taoist Canon.

Ch'ing (Qing) dynasty

1644–1911

NOTES

CHAPTER 2: Foundations

1 Adapted from Wing-tsit Chan, trans. and comp., *A Source Book in Chinese Philosophy* (Princeton, N.J.: Princeton University Press, 1963), 209.

CHAPTER 3: Scriptures

2 The Analects, 7:16.

3 Wing-tsit Chan, *A Source Book in Chinese Philosophy*, 180.

4 In some versions, the man's name was Yü Chi (Yu Ji), because the Chinese characters for "kan" and "yü" look very similar.

CHAPTER 4: Worldview

5 D.C. Lau, trans., *Lao Tzu: Tao Te Ching* (Harmondsworth, U.K.: Penguin Books, 1963), 82.

6 Wing-tsit Chan, *A Source Book in Chinese Philosophy*, 194.

7 Lau, *Lao Tzu*, 64.

8 Ibid., 65.

9 Adapted from Lau, *Lao Tzu*, 67.

10 The "magic number" of five also appears in Confucian categorizations, though their correspondence to the Five Elements are not clearly identified. There are five respectful ones: Heaven, Earth, Ruler, Parents, and Teachers. There are five basic human relationships: the relationship between the ruler and the ruled, between father and son, between husband and wife, between older brother and younger brother, and between friends.

CHAPTER 6: Growing Up Taoist

11 Rat, ox, tiger, rabbit, dragon, serpent, horse, goat, monkey, rooster, dog, and pig.

CHAPTER 7: Cultural Expressions

12 Adapted from Kristofer Schipper, "Taoism: the Story of the Way," in *Taoism and the Arts of China*, edited by Stephen Little and Shawn Eichman (Chicago, Ill.: The Art Institute of Chicago, 2000), 46.

13 Paul W. Kroll, "Body Gods and Inner Vision: The Scripture of the Yellow Court," in *Religions of China in Practice*, edited by Donald S. Lopez, Jr. (Princeton, N.J.: Princeton University Press, 1996), 149–55.

CHAPTER 8: Holidays

14 In some regions it is on the second day of the first month on the lunar calendar.

15 Usually during the *Yin* time (from 3 A.M. to 5 A.M.), or the *Mao* time (from 5 A.M. to 7 A.M. in the morning). For more information concerning the Chinese double-hour system, please see the sidebar in chapter 8.

CHAPTER 9: Memories

16 "The Yin-Yang doctrine is very simple but its influence has been extensive. No aspect of Chinese civilization—whether metaphysics, medicine, government, or art—has escaped its imprint. . . . The two concepts of the yin yang and the Five Agents go far back to antiquity and to quite independent origins. . . . Briefly, both the yin yang and the Five Agents doctrines may be regarded as early Chinese attempts in the direction of working out a metaphysics and a cosmology." Wing-tsit Chan, trans. and comp., *A Source Book in Chinese Philosophy* (Princeton, N.J.: Princeton University Press, 1973), 244–45. Yin-Yang and Five-phases theories had long been discussed in various Pre-Ch'in works, but the systematic account of it was mainly developed in the Han era.

17 "Taoism was from the beginning to end a natural outgrowth of native ways of thought and action." Timothy Hugh Barrett, *Taoism under the T'ang: Religion and Empire during the Golden Age of Chinese History* (London: Wellsweep Press, 1996), 17.

CHAPTER 10: Taoism in the World Today

18 "Animism" is no longer in vogue as a religious category. The evolutionary model that ranked religions from "primitive" to "high," and placed "animism" among the "primitive" religions, is no longer used by credible religious theorists. The evolutionary model of religions was overtly biased against non-Western and non-monotheistic traditions.

GLOSSARY

Chang Tao-ling (Zhang Daoling) (second century C.E.)—Founded the first religious Taoist organization during the Eastern Han dynasty and is revered as the "Heavenly Master" (T'ien-shih).

Chuang-tzu (Zhuangzi) (traditional dates: 369–286 B.C.E.)—Thinker living in the Warring States period. He is generally regarded as the second most prominent figure in Taoism, philosophical or religious. The book Chuang-tzu, otherwise called Nan-hua Ching, is ascribed to him.

Emperor Hsüan (Xuan) of the T'ang (Tang) dynasty (r. 712–756 C.E.)—Famous emperor who was probably the most pious Taoist among all of the emperors of the T'ang dynasty. Besides ordering the Taoist Canon to be compiled for the first time, he also composed music for Taoist rituals.

feng shui—Form of geomancy that utilizes the Eight Trigrams of the Book of Change (I-Ching), as well as Taoist theories of Yin-Yang and the Five Elements.

geomancy—Method of situating homes in order to maximize beneficial effects from the energy in the sky and environment.

Huang-ti (Huangdi)—Legendary figure who is said to be the common ancestor of the Chinese people. At the beginning of the Han dynasty his name was mentioned together with Lao-tzu, as in the "Method of Huang and Lao" and the "Way of Huang and Lao." Many Taoist scriptures are attributed to him.

I-Ching (Yijing)—Scripture commonly translated as the Book of Change. It explains the meaning for every line of each of the sixty-four hexagrams, which are formed by putting the Eight Trigrams on top of each other. Both Confucians and Taoists honor this scripture as one of their sacred texts.

kan-chih (ganzhi)—Combines the abbreviations for "t'ien-kan/tian'gan" (heavenly stems) and "ti-chih/dizhi" (earthly branches). T'ien-kan and ti-chih are two different sets of counters used by Chinese, the former containing ten "stems" and the latter twelve "branches."

Combined together they form a cycle of sixty (the t'ien-kan always precedes the ti-chih in the combination), which is frequently used to count years.

Kuan-yin (Guanyin)—the Bodhisattva Avalokiteśvara. For Chinese and Japanese, the bodhisattva takes the female form and is depicted as a mother-like figure who will come to the rescue of all those who suffer and call up to her. Taoists recognize her as one of the Taoist deities, though obviously the idea of a bodhisattva comes from Buddhism.

Lao-tzu (Laozi) (sixth century B.C.E.)—Thinker who lived in the Spring and Autumn period. Believed to be the author of the Tao Te Ching, he is commonly honored as the founder of Taoism and is deified by Taoists. The royal families of the T'ang dynasty traced their ancestry to him.

Lieh-hsien chuan (Liexianzhuan)—Hagiographical text in Taoism, translated as the Record of Immortals. Written in the Han dynasty, it contains the legends of about seventy immortals of previous times, such as Huang-ti and Lao-tzu.

Lung-Shan Temple (Longshan Temple)—Temple located in Taipei, Taiwan; it fully demonstrates the Taoist spirit of inclusivism, because Taoists worship deities of different origins here.

Nan-hua Ching (Nanhuajing)—Another name for the book Chuang-tzu—the second most important text in both philosophical and religious Taoism. It is commonly attributed to Chuang-tzu, though some scholars consider it a collaborative work.

pa-kua (bagua)—The Eight Trigrams that stand for sky, earth, mountain, lake, fire, water, thunder, and wind. The pa-kua is the foundation of the feng shui practice; each of these Trigrams is associated with a color, an aspect of life, a family member, and/or a group of materials.

Sheng-jen (Shengren)—Chinese term for "sage." In Tao Te Ching, this term usually refers to the ideal ruler.

T'ai-chi (Taiji)—Literally the "Supreme Ultimate"; cosmic whole that combines and yet transcends the Yin and the Yang or any sort of dichotomies. The term is also used to refer to a kind of Chinese martial arts that is known for its slow and smooth movements.

T'ai-p'ing Ching (Taipingjing)—Scripture of the Ultimate Equilibrium. It first appeared around the beginning of the Common Era and is the first religious Taoist scripture available. A religious Taoist organization that emerged during the Eastern Han dynasty revered this scripture as its canon and acquired its name, "T'ai-p'ing Tao," because of this fact.

Tao-shih (Daoshi)—Chinese word for professional Taoists, who were also called fang-shih at the inception of religious Taoism. The fang-shih were believed to have the knowledge or power to communicate with the supernatural world. Later the term is used to refer to those who devote their life to Taoist practices and ideals, and/or to those who know how to perform Taoist rituals in events such as funerals or the celebrations of some deities' birthdays.

Tao-tsang (Daozang)—Taoist Canon. It refers to the collection of Taoist scriptures from various vintages. It was first compiled during the reign of Emperor Hsüan of the T'ang dynasty and was compiled another six times in Chinese history.

Tao Te Ching (Daodejing)—Commonly translated as the Classic of the Way and Its Power. It is the single most revered scripture in both philosophical and religious Taoism, and is traditionally attributed to Lao-tzu, though some scholars think it was written by a group of thinkers.

T'ien-shih Tao (Tianshi Dao)—"Way of the Heavenly Master"; it is the first religious Taoist organization founded by Chang Tao-ling in the early Eastern Han dynasty.

Tsou Yen (Zou Yan) (c. 305–240 B.C.E)—Sole representative of the *Yin-Yang*ism in the Pre-Ch'in Era that is known now.

Wu-hsing (Wuxing)—Chinese word for the Five Elements (Forces, Agents, Phases, Stages): Wood, Fire, Earth, Metal, and Water. There exist mutually enhancing and mutually weakening relationships among the five. Taoists used to understand the natural and human phenomena in the world in terms of these five categories. The Five-Element theory is one of the bases for feng shui.

Yü-huang shang-ti (Yuhuang shangdi)—More widely known as the Jade Emperor by English speakers, he is commonly believed to be the supreme deity and the ruler of all other Taoist deities, though professional Taoists may not necessarily think so.

BIBLIOGRAPHY

Barrett, Timothy Hugh. *Taoism under the T'ang: Religion and Empire During the Golden Age of Chinese History.* London: Wellsweep Press, 1996.

Chan, Wing-tsit, trans. and comp. *A Source Book in Chinese Philosophy.* Princeton, N.J.: Princeton University Press, 1963.

Ching, Julia. *Chinese Religions.* Maryknoll, N.Y.: Orbis Books, 1993.

Gregory, Peter N., and Patricia Buckley Ebrey. "The Religious and Historical Landscape." In *Religion and Society in T'ang and Sung China,* edited by Patricia Buckley Ebrey and Peter N. Gregory, pp. 1–44. Honolulu, Hawaii: University of Hawaii Press, 1993.

Kaltenmark, Max. "The Ideology of the T'ai-p'ing ching." In *Facets of Taoism: Essays in Chinese Religion,* edited by Holmes Welch and Anna Seidel, pp. 19–45. New Haven, Conn.: Yale University Press, 1979.

Lau, D.C., trans. *Lao Tzu: Tao Te Ching.* Harmondsworth, U.K.: Penguin Books, 1963.

Little, Stephen, and Shawn Eichman, comp. *Taoism and the Arts of China.* Chicago, Ill.: The Art Institute of Chicago, 2000.

Lopez, Donald S., Jr. *Religions of China in Practice.* Princeton, N.J.: Princeton University Press, 1996.

Stein, Rolf A. "Religious Taoism and Popular Religion from the Second to Seventh Centuries." In *Facets of Taoism: Essays in Chinese Religion,* edited by Holmes Welch and Anna Seidel, pp. 53–81. New Haven, Conn.: Yale University Press, 1979.

Wilkinson, Endymion. *Chinese History: A Manual,* revised and enlarged edition. Cambridge, Mass: Harvard University Press, 2000.

FURTHER READING

Blofeld, John. *Taoism.* Boston, Mass.: Shambhala, 2000.

Kirkland, Russell. *Taoism: The Enduring Tradition.* New York: Routledge, 2004.

Lau, D.C., trans. *Lao Tzu: Tao Te Ching.* Harmondsworth, U.K.: Penguin Books, 1963.

Oldstone-Moore, Jennifer. *Taoism: Origins, Beliefs, Practices, Holy Texts, Sacred Places.* New York: Oxford University Press, 2003.

Porter, John M. *The Tao of Star Wars.* Atlanta, Ga.: Humanics Trade Group, 2003.

WEBSITES

Chinese Festivals and Holidays
http://www.c-c-c.org/chineseculture/festival/festival.html

Chinese Zodiac
http://www.chinatoday.com/culture/zodiac/zodiac.htm

Eight Trigrams
http://www.littlestcat.com/iching/Trigrams.html

Taoist Deities
http://www.ankhoaagency.com/taoist_deities.htm

Taoism Depot
http://www.edepot.com/taoism.html

Taoism Information Page
http://www.clas.ufl.edu/users/gthursby/taoism

Taoist Talismans
http://eng.taoism.org.hk/religious-activities&rituals/talismans-registers&magic-skills/pg4-3-1-2.asp

Page:

B: (top) © Burstein Collection/ CORBIS

B: (bottom) © Robert Mulder/ Ponkawonka.com

C: (top) © Royalty-Free/CORBIS

C: (bottom) © HIP/Scala/ Art Resource, NY

D: © Image Select/ Art Resource, NY

E: © Julia Waterlow, Eye Ubiquitous/CORBIS

F: © Royal Ontario Museum/ CORBIS

G: © HIP/Scala/ Art Resource, NY

H: ©Réunion des Musées Nationaux/Art Resource, NY

Cover: © Philadelphia Museum of Art/CORBIS

CONTRIBUTORS

HSIAO-LAN HU is a native of the Republic of China (Taiwan), where she studied feng shui and the Book of Change (I-Ching). Ms. Hu has a B.A. in philosophy from National Taiwan University, an M.A. in Religion from the University of Iowa, and is currently a Ph.D. candidate in Religion at Temple University.

WILLIAM CULLY ALLEN, Ph.D., is Professor of Religion at Temple University, where he teaches graduate courses in Hinduism and Indian Buddhism and an undergraduate survey of Asian Religions, including Taoism and Confucianism. He has published articles in the *Hindu-Christian Studies Bulletin* and the *Journal of Dharma.* Dr. Allen is also a tennis professional teaching at the Cherry Hill (New Jersey) Health and Racquet Club, and is now preparing to publish a book entitled *The Tao of Tennis.*

ANN MARIE B. BAHR is professor of religious studies at South Dakota State University. Her areas of teaching, research, and writing include World Religions, New Testament, Religion in American Culture, and the Middle East. Her articles have appeared in *Annual Editions: World Religions 03/04* (Guilford, Conn.: McGraw-Hill, 2003), *The Journal of Ecumenical Studies,* and *Covenant for a New Creation: Ethics, Religion and Public Policy* (Maryknoll, N.Y.: Orbis, 1991). Since 1999, she has authored a weekly newspaper column which analyzes the cultural significance of religious holidays. She has served as president of the Upper Midwest Region of the American Academy of Religion.

MARTIN E. MARTY, an ordained minister in the Evangelical Lutheran Church in America, is the Fairfax M. Cone Distinguished Service Professor Emeritus at the University of Chicago Divinity School, where he taught for thirty-five years. Marty has served as president of the American Academy of Religion, the American Society of Church History, and the American Catholic Historical Association, and was also a member of two U.S. presidential commissions. He is currently Senior Regent at St. Olaf College in Northfield, Minnesota. Marty has written more than fifty books, including the three-volume *Modern American Religion* (University of Chicago Press). His book *Righteous Empire* was a recipient of the National Book Award.